THE HERITAGE OF INDIA SERIES

A HISTORY OF TELUGU LITERATURE

THE HERITAGE OF INDIA SERIES

A HISTORY OF TELUGU LITERATURE

BY

P. CHENCHIAH, M L.

AND

RAJA M. BHUJANGA RAO BAHADUR

FOREWORD

BY

THE HONBLE MR. C.R. REDDY, M.A.

VICE CHANCELLOR OF THE ANDHRA UNIVERSITY

GYAN

Published by

GYAN

Gyan Publishing House
5, Ansari Road
Daryaganj, New Delhi-110002
Phone: 011-47034999, 9811692060
E-mail: books@gyanbooks.com

Distribution Network
gyanbooks.com
India, USA, Canada, UK, Australia, France

ISBN : 978-81-212-4524-1 (HB)

2nd Impression 2020

Printed at: Gyan Press, Delhi.

The book at your disposal is the edition of an old book originally published long back. The Text quality of this book may not be at par as compared to our other books but many readers approached us to reprint this important book so that it could satiate their hunger. We request all the readers of this book to help us to improve its quality by providing the necessary text of those pages which are not properly visible. Your valuable support in this case will be highly appreciated and acknowledged and our future readers will be benefitted immensely.

DEDICATION :

KRĪSTĀRPAṆAM

FOREWORD

I HAVE cursorily glanced through the *History of Telugu Literature* by Mr. Chenchiah and Raja Bhujanga Rao, and have been much struck by the authors' grasp of the subject and broad illuminating views.

Mr. Rice's book on *Kanarese Literature* opened what to South Indians must have appeared as a new way of treating literary histories; and the present authors have benefited to the full by Mr. Rice's example. Doubtless the critical student may find in this work occasional omissions, which are inevitable in view of the enormous growth of new matter as a result of recent events and researches.

Vīraśaiva literature is now being reclaimed. And if the libraries of the various mutts of His Exalted Highness in the Nizam's Dominions are ransacked, it is very likely that more books belonging to the same group may be discovered, as also perhaps books having a special bearing on Buddhism and Jainism. The ruthless manner in which Buddhist and Jain literature, in Sanskrit as well as the vernaculars, was suppressed and destroyed through the Brahminical reaction is the greatest tragedy of Indian culture. Today, much of that vast treasure has to be imported from Tibetan and Chinese renderings. Though the outlook as regards possible finds in our own country is almost blank, I am still in hopes of occasional good fortune in this line, if a diligent and systematic search is instituted.

One of the merits of the present work is the historical background presented, and the suggestive manner in which literature is linked up with the general social and political history of the Āndhra Dēśa. Literature is life, either in its growth or its decadence; and unless it is correlated with life, it cannot be properly appreciated. And literature is, not infrequently, propaganda. Years ago, I suggested that the real motive underlying the translation of the *Mahābhārata* into Telugu, with all its pro-Brahminical interpolations, was propaganda through the vernaculars, as a counterblast to the Buddhist and Jain propaganda, which all through was carried through Māgadhī and other vernaculars of India. Indeed, Errāpragada, in one of his verses, suggests that his illustrious predecessors, Nanniah and Tikkanna, undertook the translation of the *Mahābhārata* in order to rectify the erroneous views that were widely prevalent. These 'erroneous views' could have been only the Jain version of the *Mahābhārata*, popular in the Kannaḍa language, with which in its early days Telugu seems to have had a closer relationship than at present, as is to be inferred from the fact that a number of Āndhras were the pioneers in Kannaḍa literature and grammar, and that poets of the distinguished rank of Nannechōdu Nāchana Soma, and Nārāyaṇa Bhaṭ were celebrated for their attainments in Kanarese. In Jain literature, the *Mahābhārata* appears under the name of Ārjuna Vijaya. It is a frankly secular poem, in which there is hardly any trace of the deification of Kṛishṇa.

The kernel of the *Mahābhārata* seems to have been an ancient book famous under the name of *Jaya*. And how this simple book *Jaya* expanded into the encyclopædia of the post-Āraṇyaka, but pre-Purāṇic, Aryan civilisation has yet to be investigated. When I say 'pre-Purāṇic,' I am not unmindful of still later interpolations, pertaining to the worship of Śiva and Vishṇu, such as the *Daśavatāra Stōtra* by Bhishma, interpolated in the *Śānti Parva*.

Similarly, there is a Jain version of the *Rāmāyaṇa* which is very different from the poem of Vālmīki. If it is further remembered that in the *Kathā Sarit Sāgara* ('the Ocean of Indian Legends') the stories of the *Mahābhārata*, *Rāmāyaṇa*, and *Bhāgavata* do not figure prominently, the idea must suggest itself to any historical student that here is a vast field of research, with a view to find out how and when, for what reasons, and with what objects, the legendary lore of Hindu India developed into its present form.

Unfortunately, this wider field of cultural investigation is beyond the scope of the present book, which deals only with Telugu literature. And Telugu literature is to a certain extent, though not to such a large extent as hasty critics imagine, imitative of Sanskrit.

A separate history may have to be written on the indigenous elements in Telugu literature, such as the lyrics or Paṭalū, the Yaksha Gānams or village dramas, and the great reformer-poets, like Vemana, a star of the first magnitude in our firmament, and all those who have given expression to the true Telugu spirit and soul. Men of genius like Kona Buddha Reddy, the author of the *Rāmāyaṇa*, which has been spuriously attributed to a mythical Raṅganātha, were able to Dravidianise the *Rāmāyaṇa* itself. A critical comparison with the poem of Vālmīki would reveal how deftly and with what consummate art Kona Buddha Reddy incorporated South Indian legends into that Aryan poem, and with what passion and imagination he treated those soul-stirring themes. The story of Sulochana and the legend of Rameśvaram, the story of Rāvana's *Pātāḷa Homam*, and the magnificent manner in which he executes the arresting transfiguration of Angada, Mandodari and Tāra are amongst the instances in point. No mere bilingual pandit could have given us Kona Buddha's rendering, which is so popular as to have become the domestic possession of every family in the Ceded Districts.

Perhaps there is also a geographical distinction between the Telugu literature of the Aryanised 'Circars,' and the predominantly Dravidian 'Ceded Districts.' If lists of works produced are prepared on a geographical basis, this distinction will come into relief. Nor can we omit from the catalogue of the books expressive of the true Āndhra soul, ballads like *Palnāti Vīracharitra*, attributed to Śrīnātha.

If I may venture on an observation, I rather think that, under the influence of a robust nationalism and Bengali literature, the Telugu soul is again finding itself in its own literature, and expressing itself in its varied moods and accents. The number of contemporary men of genius seems to be very large, and the varieties of literature produced are also large. Simplicity of expression, sincerity of emotion, natural figures of speech are again becoming the prevalent literary mode, and our literature has emerged from the unnaturalisms and idiosyncracies of the Prabandha period, which is the period, generally speaking, of our decadence.

How I wish that some competent scholar, with enough sympathy and imagination in him, would write an exhaustive history of contemporary literature, of the social drama, the lyrics, the narrative poems, the satires, the social and psychological novels, the humorous stories, the histories, etc., which have been added to our literature within the last twenty-five years.

I welcome the present book as one of the best of its kind—and, considering how rare that kind is, as a most important contribution to the history of Telugu literature. I trust that this will encourage further histories being attempted, and also histories dealing with special periods or special subjects.

C. R. REDDY.

PREFACE

This volume is the first attempt in English, and probably indeed in any language, to present to the reader a concise and continuous history of Telugu literature. It is too much to hope that such a book can escape the limitations and defects incidental to a first effort. Our object has been not only to make a comprehensive inventory of poets and their productions and to supply accurate information, but also so to reconstruct the past as to enable the reader to assess the literary heritage of the Telugu people at its true worth. With this object in view, we have given concise biographical details of the Telugu poets, critical estimates of standard Telugu works, and a general survey of Telugu literary tendencies, in their proper historical setting. The chapter dealing with contemporary literature is of necessity incomplete, but we hope enough has been said to show the promise for the future which the intellectual ferment of the last few decades holds. The views expressed in 'Retrospect and Prospect' are put forward as our own, though the approval of a large and rapidly growing school of literary men can be claimed for them. For dates and authorship, we have on the whole followed the lead of Mr. Vīresalingam, except where later research demanded departure.

Where obligations are extensive and varied it is invidious to particularise. We should like to place on record our special indebtedness to Mr. Vīresalingam and Mr. Vanguri Subba Rao, among authors, and to the *Āndhra Parishad Patrika*, and *Bhāratī*, among periodicals. Our thanks are also due to friends who have read through the book in manuscript and offered their valuable suggestions and criticisms.

EDITORIAL PREFACE

> Finally, brethren, whatsoever things are true, whatsoever things are honourable, whatsoever things are just, whatsoever things are pure, whatsoever things are lovely, whatsoever things are of good report; if there be any virtue, and if there be any praise, think on these things.

No section of the population of India can afford to neglect her ancient heritage. The treasures of knowledge, wisdom, and beauty which are contained in her literature, philosophy, art, and regulated life are too precious to be lost. Every citizen of India needs to use them, if he is to be a cultured modern Indian. This is as true of the Christian, the Muslim, the Zoroastrian as of the Hindu. But, while the heritage of India has been largely explored by scholars, and the results of their toil are laid out for us in books, they cannot be said to be really available for the ordinary man. The volumes are in most cases expensive, and are often technical and difficult. Hence this series of cheap books has been planned by a group of Christian men, in order that every educated Indian, whether rich or poor, may be able to find his way into the treasures of India's past. Many Europeans, both in India and elsewhere, will doubtless be glad to use the series.

The utmost care is being taken by the General Editors in selecting writers, and in passing manuscripts for the press. To every book two tests are rigidly applied: everything must be scholarly, and everything must be sympathetic. The purpose is to bring the best out of the ancient treasuries, so that it may be known, enjoyed, and used.

CONTENTS

I

INTRODUCTORY

TELUGU is one of the four important languages that are spoken in South India, the other three being Tamil, Malayalam and Kanarese. According to the Census of 1921, the Telugu-speaking people number 23½ millions in the whole of India, 18 millions of whom inhabit a continuous block of territory, 117,000 square miles in extent. A semicircle, drawn with the line joining Rajahmundry and Madras as diameter, includes most of the Telugu country. Within this area are to be found a considerable number of Muhammadans and a sprinkling of naturalised Tamils known as Podur Dravidas. In almost every district of South India Telugus numbering over many thousands are to be found. They are the descendants of the colonists who settled in Tamil-land, when that country was ruled by the Telugu emperor, Kṛishṇadevarāya of Vijayanagar, and the deputies appointed by him. The Presidency of Bombay, and the Native States of Mysore and Hyderabad, contain a Telugu population of nearly six millions in all. It is said that those who add 'Telang' to their names in the Bombay Presidency are of Telugu extraction. The Telugus are an enterprising people and were among the first in India to emigrate to countries outside, such as Java; in recent years they have migrated in large numbers to Burma and Assam.

Origins. The origins of a people and their language are largely matters of speculation, incapable of certainty. Many writers on ethnology hold that the Dravidian races of South India were the inhabitants of the country before the Aryan invasions and that in race and culture they are unrelated to the Aryans; but this theory, so far as the Telugus are concerned, is purely of antiquarian interest. The Telugus may have been in the remote past a Dravidian people possessing a non-Aryan culture, but they seem to have lost their Dravidian identity very early in their history. In historical times they were so completely Aryanised in religion, language and literature, that for all practical purposes they may be treated as Aryans; although the indigenous Dravidian influence continued to make itself felt.

Andhra Desa—*the land ot the Āndhras.* The classic and historic name for the people now known as Telugus is Āndhras, a word which is variously derived, but almost all the derivations contain the idea of darkness. It is generally believed that the territory originally inhabited by the Āndhras was a part of Daṇḍakāraṇya of the *Rāmāyaṇa*, a dark and inaccessible region in the wild forests of South India. In the *Aitreya Brāhmaṇa*, *Rāmāyaṇa*, *Mahābhārata* and *Skanda Purāṇa*, the term is used as referring to a race. In one place in the *Rāmāyaṇa* it has a territorial significance. The *Bhāgavata* states that the country was named after King Āndhrudu. The early references on the whole make 'Āndhra' to be the appellation of a race, and we may take it that the name was first applied to a people, who in turn impressed it on the country they lived in, and on the language they spoke.

Āndhra Deśa was also known as Veṅgī Deśa. It is, however, probable that Veṅgī was a part of the Telugu country—the part which lay between the Godāvarī and the Kṛishṇa. The name 'Triliṅga' was often applied to the Telugu country. This may have been used to signify either the country which contains the three shrines (liṅgas), namely, those at Kāleśvaraṁ, Śrī Śailaṁ and Draksha Rāmam, or the country between these shrines. The suggestion that 'Triliṅga' is a contraction for *Trikaliṅga* does not appear to be sound. For administrative and other purposes the country was differently divided at different times. The earliest division was into *Vishayās*; a later one was into *Nādūs*, the modern one being into 'Districts.' As references to Nādūs are of frequent occurrence in literature, it may be useful to notice the prominent Nādūs:

1. *Veṅgī Nādū*, the territory between the Godāvarī and

the Kṛishṇa, which was the original homeland of the Telugus, with its capital at Rajahmundry.

2. *Muliki Nādū*, beginning with the Cuddappah District and extending to Mysore.

3. *Pottipi Nādū*, from Cuddappah to Pennar.

4. *Renādū* and *Mānādū*, Kurnool District.

5. *Palnādū*, West of Guntur.

6. *Pākanādū*, the coastal tract from Nellore to Kṛishṇa.

7. *Kammanādū*, in Guntur District, from Konidena to Kammamettu.

8. *Velinādū*, in Guntur District, with Chandavolu as capital.

Andhras. Like the Aryans, the Āndhras are divided into four castes: 'Chatur Varna'—Brahmins, Kshatriyas, Vaiśyas and Śūdras. The Brahmins fall under two main heads: Vaidikīs, those who once followed the priestly profession; and Niyogīs, the laity. The Kshatriyas among Telugus are represented by the Rāchavāru. The Śūdras are subdivided into Velamās, Reddis, Balijās and Kāpus. Beneath these there is a large submerged population of Pañchamas. It is interesting to note that while literary writers are not restricted to one class or section of the society, the honour of making by far the largest contribution belongs to the Niyogīs. The Kshatriyas and the Reddis have been patrons of art. The Dvijās or Twice-born among Telugus follow the Vedic ceremonies and Aryan Saṁskāras. In religion, the Telugus have been, on the whole, staunch adherents of Hinduism in its three later variations—Advaitism; Śaṅkara's Śaivism, including Liṅgāyatism; and Vaishṇavism. Jainism and Buddhism, though they have gained temporary successes, did not leave any abiding mark on the people or their literature. The same may be said of Muhammadanism and, in some measure, of Christianity.

Andhra Bhasha—*the language of the Āndhras.* This is known as Telugu, or *Tenugu* (*tene* = honey, *agu* = is), meaning, sweet as honey. Telugu is numbered among the Dravidian languages, of which four are of importance in South India, namely, Tamil, Telugu, Malayalam and Kanarese. Dr. Caldwell, in his *Comparative Grammar*, has given currency to the theory that they are unrelated to Sanskrit. Sharply opposed to this theory is the view, maintained by all Telugu grammarians and Sanskrit philologists, that Telugu is Vikṛitī—that is, a language formed by the modification of Sanskrit and *Prākṛit.* An analysis of the language as it has been for centuries confirms this traditional view. Dr. Caldwell's view may be true, if applied to the condition of the language at its origin; while the traditional view accounts for its present form. There are groups of words in the language, which are common to Telugu and other Dravidian languages, indicating their descent from a common parent in the remote past. It would appear that very early the Āndhras adopted a form of Prākṛit which, in the course of development, became the immediate ancestor of Telugu and Kanarese, aptly termed Kanarese-Telugu by Dr. Caldwell. From this archetype the differentiation into the modern Telugu and modern Kanarese must have taken place. For this view there is ample justification in the vocabulary and the syntax of the language. Telugu contains very few original words of its own. Its vocabulary is classified by grammarians under five heads:

1. *Tatsamamulu*, Sanskrit equivalents.
2. *Tadbhavamulu*, Sanskrit derivatives.
3. *Deśīyamulu*, indigenous words.
4. *Anyamulu*, foreign words.

Many words in Telugu are 'synthetic'—that is, are made up of initial letters of Dravidian languages and final letters of North Indian tongues. This composite structure indicates that people of many races have met, in the Godāvarī-Kṛishṇa Delta, under the stress of historic circumstances, and were fused into a single community. The language, also, was evolved when the racial fusion was taking place.

The Telugu language does not seem to be as ancient as Tamil, though it is more ancient than Malayāḷam, and at least of equal antiquity with Kanarese. It is not possible to say with any certainty when the language now known as Telugu came into vogue. There is no available literature before the eleventh century A.D. All the inscriptions before this period are either in Prākṛit or Sanskrit. The Āndhras ruled practically the whole of middle India in the beginning of the Christian era. But the information at our disposal does not enable us to say whether they used Telugu in any form. It is probable that they spoke a form of Prākṛit, from which Telugu has descended.

The lack of antiquity in the Telugu language is felt as a reproach by some writers, who believe that the greatness of a language depends on its age. This has given rise to later legends, one of which, tracing the origin of Telugu to the fourth quarter of *Kṛita Yuga* (the Golden Age), is as follows: Agnimitra lost his eyes owing to excessive heat. He prayed to the sun-god, who, pleased with his devotion, taught him a language so potent that it restored him his eyesight. This language was called Āndhra *Bhāshā*, as it dispelled darkness. We are also told that each *yuga* had its particular form of Telugu and that in *Kāli Yuga* (the Present Age), Kaliṅga Āndhra and Raudra Āndhra were established by Nandivardhana and his disciple, Devaḷa Rāya, in the reign of Śātakarṇi.

Andhra Lipi—*the Telugu script.* In its current form this was stereotyped about the thirteenth century A.D. Palæologists have traced the growth of Telugu script from remote ancestry. About the fourth century B.C. a type of character known as *Brāhmī Lipi* was evolved in Northern India, and gradually spread to the southern portion of the continent under the name of *Draviḍa Brāhmī*. This Dravidian Brāhmī, different in some respects from the Mauryan script of Aśoka inscriptions, is the common parent of all South Indian scripts. It has undergone modifications in different places and at different times, of which we may mention a few important variations that are in the line of modern Telugu script. One modification is found in the Guha Śāsanas (cave edicts) of the Āndhra kings, another in the inscriptions of Veṅgī Deśa, the original homeland of the Telugus. There is not much difference between the Guha and Veṅgī Lipis. The letters are crooked, though curvilinear. In the time of the Chāḷukyā kings we find a further change in the characters. It is in the eleventh century A.D. that we find the script taking a shape which, to the untrained eye, seems to have clear affinity to modern characters; and Nanniah, the first poet of the Telugu language, wrote in these characters. Between A.D. 1000–1300 Telugu and Kanarese had the same script; but about the time of Tikkanna the Telugu characters separated themselves from the Kanarese, and assumed their current shapes. A theory is propounded that the letters of the Telugu alphabets are all carved out of a circle. This view, though not historical, may not be altogether fanciful. The beautiful circular final form of the present alphabet is, probably, due to the influence of this view.

Telugu has a complete and scientific system of letters to express sounds and is phonetically satisfactory. It has more letters than any other Dravidian language, some of them specially introduced to express fine shades of difference in sounds. We have full zero (*Anusvāra*), half-zero (*Arthānusvāra*) and *Visarga* to express the various shades of nasal sounds. L and Ḷ, R and Ṛ are differentiated; we have a CH and JH, which are not represented in Sanskrit, and an S, SH, and KSH, not found in Tamil. Telugu has made its letters expressive of all the sounds it had to deal with, borrowing from Sanskrit, Tamil, and Hindustani, when necessary.

Sources. The sources for the history of Telugu literature are:

1. *The Prologues to the Poems.* Following the Sanskrit model, it is customary for the Telugu poets to give in each introduction a genealogy of the writer, the history of the king to whom the book is dedicated and of the dynasty to which he belongs, the names of the books composed by the author, and the names of the important earlier poets in chronological order. Valuable historical information can be extracted from this source.

2. *Inscriptions.* Telugu literature is concerned more with local history than with the major movements of Indian conquests. It is to the inscriptions that we are indebted for detailed information as to the history and chronology of the events referred to in the poems.

3. *Grammars and Anthologies.* There are several grammars, treatises on poetics, and anthologies, which give illustrative stanzas from the poets of the day. As many as one hundred poets, otherwise unknown, have

been recovered from oblivion through references in these treatises.

4. *Tradition.* Though not of much value as history, the importance of tradition for recovering the atmosphere and local colour cannot be over-estimated. Tradition also embodies a critical impression of the poets, some illuminating biographical touches, and a large fund of interesting anecdotes.

5. *Lives of Poets*, and histories of literature, written in the vernacular by authors of ripe scholarship and critical acumen, furnish in an intelligible form the net results of modern research.

Periods of Telugu Literature. The usual division is the chronological one, into early, middle and modern epochs. This classification is unsatisfactory, as it gives too much importance to the decadent period and too little to the modern renaissance. A division based on literary modes and tendencies is also sometimes adopted. This gives us four periods:

1. The period of translation.
2. The period of expansion.
3. The period of abridgement.
4. The period of imitation.

If we combine these two classifications, we may divide the history of Telugu literature into the following periods:

1. The period of early beginnings.
2. The period of translations.
3. The Prabandha period.
4. The period of decadence.
5. The modern renaissance;

and this classification will be adopted in the following pages.

II

HISTORICAL AND RELIGIOUS BACKGROUND

THE Āndhras have an ancient and illustrious history, though the beginning of the race is clouded in legend and mystery. In the *Rāmāyaṇa* and *Mahābhārata* they are referred to as a primitive tribe, inhabiting the wild and inaccessible southern forest, Daṇḍakāraṇya. The inscriptions of Aśoka mention them as a community on the fringes of the empire. During the decline and fall of the Maurya Dynasty, the Āndhra 'protected state' was among the earliest areas to revolt; and it rapidly grew into a powerful independent kingdom, stretching right across the middle of India, with its base touching the great Tamil kingdoms in the south. There were two great branches of the Āndhras; the sovereign, ruling over the eastern territories with his capital at Dhānyakaṭaka; and the heir-apparent, governing the western dominions, residing at Paithan. The Āndhra period was one of considerable prosperity. After a duration of four and a half centuries, Āndhra dominion came to an end about the middle of the third century A.D., though it is not known how or why. It is a remarkable instance of national loss of memory that Telugu literature is silent of the glories of the Āndhra Empire. The kings and heroes of this period are not celebrated in epic, *kāvya* or song. As far as Telugu literature is concerned, the Āndhra Empire might as well not have existed at all. The only memory of the Āndhra kings, dimly echoed in this literature, is associated with the seventeenth king of the dynasty, who is either the author or *Krutipati* of *Saptaśatī* in Prākṛit. Śrīnātha says that, in the prime of his youth, he translated *Sālivāhana Saptaśatī*, but the book has not come down to us. There is also the tradition that a Kāṇva composed a Telugu grammar, just as Agastya is said to have composed the first Tamil grammar. When we remember that the Āndhras succeeded the Kāṇva Dynasty, we may reasonably conjecture that this Kāṇva was a member of the supplanted dynasty, and that his grammar was in Prākṛit.

The Āndhras were Buddhists by religion, and it is possible that the literature of the day existed in Prākṛit, one form of which is considered to be the immediate literary ancestor of Telugu. The Pallavās, who conquered the country, must have exterminated Buddhism and Buddhistic literature, of which not a vestige has survived.

The immediate conquerors of the Āndhras were the Pallavās, who seem to have risen to power suddenly in the south. Starting from Kāñchī, their capital, they extended their empire northwards till it included Veṅgī Nādū. Very little is known of the Pallavās in general, or of their rule in the Āndhra country in particular. All that we can be certain of is that, after the Āndhras, they ruled the country from A.D. 230–550 and were in turn ousted by the Chāḷukyās. The early Pallavās were Jains and the country adopted the Jain faith. The only fugitive glimpses preserved for us of the Jain culture are Atharvaṇa's *Bhārata*, (said to have been burnt by Nanniah), the name of Padmakavi, and *Kavi Janāsrayam*, a treatise on poetics.

About the middle of the sixth century the Chāḷukyās, a Rajput race from Ayodhyā, imposed their power on the Deccan tableland. There were two branches of the Chāḷukyās—the western, having its capital at Badami; and the eastern at Rajahmundry. We are directly concerned with the eastern Chāḷukyās, who continued to be the rulers of Veṅgī Nādū for nearly six centuries—a period during which they were engaged in ceaseless warfare with the Pallavas, and afterwards with the Choḷas on the south, and the other branch of the Chāḷukyās on the west. The conflict with the Choḷas was eventually composed by the usual expedient of royal marriages. Vimalāditya (A.D. 1005–22), the twenty-fifth reigning sovereign of the Eastern Chāḷukyās, married the daughter of Rāja-Rāja-Choda. Rāja-Rāja-Narendra and Rāja-Rāja-Vishṇuvardhana, the son and the grandson respectively of Vimalāditya, married Choḷa princesses. Thus three generations of royal unions effected a coalition of the two great rival kingdoms; and Kulottaṅga Choḷa Deva (1063–1112) transferred the capital from Veṅgī to the south. From this time forward Veṅgī Nādū sank into a province, ruled from the south by a deputy. The result of the union with the Choḷas placed in the hands of the Chāḷukyā king, Rāja-Rāja-Narendra, an empire as extensive as that of the Āndhras in the second century. It also marked an era of peace and prosperity. It was in the reign of Rāja-Rāja-Narendra that Nanniah began the translation of the *Mahābhārata* into Telugu.

The early Chāḷukyās were Jains, but the later Chāḷukyās were champions of Hinduism, and naturally enemies of Jainism. The reforms of Śaṅkara dealt a fatal blow to the power of Jainism, and by the time of Rāja-Rāja-Narendra it is clear that the conflict had ended in the victory of the former. The opening verses of the *Mahābhārata* reveal an aggressive Hinduism in the act of consolidating its victories and taking precautions against possible attacks of the enemies in the future. The religious revival intended to achieve this end is known as the *Vaidikī* movement—a movement which, much to its credit, adopted a spiritual means of fortifying the Telugu mind in its faith. While in the Kanarese and Tamil countries the conflict had degenerated into mutual persecutions, it was the *Vaidikī* movement that gave a peaceful turn to the struggle, though it cannot be said that persecutions were altogether avoided. The first effort of the new movement was to guard against the possibility of future internecine quarrels between the followers of Śiva and Vishṇu by a judicious compromise. The Advaitic background rendered such a reconciliation possible. The devotion of the *Vaidikīs* was not directed either to Hari or Harā, but to the composite deity, Harihara-nātha. There is reason to believe that this eclectic cult had obtained extensive acceptance at the time. The other feature of the movement was to flood the country with Aryan culture, and it was in pursuance of this object that extensive translations were systematically undertaken from Sanskrit into Telugu.

The interval between the change of the capital of the Chāḷukyā-Choḷa Kingdom to the south and the establishment of the Kākatīyas in the Veṅgī Nādū, presents a confused medley of events. The deputies of Kings Kulottaṅga I and II, known as Āndhra-Chodas, seem to have carved out small provinces for themselves, and ruled them as practically independent sovereigns, with nominal allegiance to the Choḷa kings. One of these had Kandukur, in Nellore District, as his capital; another, Konidena in Guntur; yet a third, Pottipi in Pākanādū. These Āndhra-Chodas had no touch with the south, except that they cherished the name of their ancestors, and kept alive the memories of their ancestral homes. Nannechōdu (1150–70), son of Ballichoda, king of Pottipi Nādū, wrote the recently discovered *Kumāra Sambhava*—the first contribution of a naturalised southerner to Telugu literature.

The Kākatīyas of Warangal, who ruled large portions of what are now called the Nizam's Dominions, and were the feudatories of the Eastern Chāḷukyās, declared independence and by A.D. 1175 conquered the Telugu province of the Choḷa king. Pratāparudra I (1140–96), the most celebrated of the Kākatīya rulers, was a patron of letters, and himself the author of *Nītisāra*, a book on politics. Pālakuriki Somanātha was attached to his court. Buddha Rāzu, the collaborator with Raṅganātha in the production of *Dvipatha-Rāmāyaṇa*, was a Samanta or minor chief of Pratāparudra. Pratāparudra was succeeded by his brother's son, Gaṇapati Deva (1199–1257). Manumasiddhi, at whose court Tikkanna flourished, was his vassal. Gaṇapati Deva was succeeded by his daughter, Rudramma. Beddanna, author of *Sumati Śataka*, was an Āndhra Choda feudatory chief of her day. Atharvaṇa, the Jain grammarian, also belongs to this period. The last king of this dynasty, Pratāparudra II (1295–1323) was defeated and taken captive by the Delhi emperor, Ghiyaz-zid-din, in 1323. Mārana dedicated his *Mārkaṇḍeya Purāṇa* to Naya-ganna Mantri, a commander of Pratāparudra II. Vydyānātha wrote an Alaṁkāra Śāstra, by name *Pratāpa Rudrīya*, during this reign. Huḷḷaki Bhāskara, the author of *Bhāskara Rāmāyaṇa*, dedicated it to Sāhiṇimāra, a cavalry officer of the king. The early Kākatīyas were Jains, but Pratāparudra and his descendants were Vīraśaivas. This faith was a 'protestant' reaction against popular Hinduism, and was avowedly anti-Brahman, though curiously enough its founder was a Telugu Brahman, Basava. It was an aggressive propagandist faith, and obtained a considerable following among the Telugus. The literature of the twelfth century is pronouncedly Vīraśaiva. Pālakuriki Somanātha, the zealous missionary of the creed and a prolific writer, has given us the scriptures of Liṅgāyatism, *Basava Purāṇa, and Paṇḍitārādhya Charita.*

Out of the ruins of the Kākatīya kingdom three principalities arose, which exercised an important influence on Telugu literature.

1. **The Reddi Dynasty** (A.D. 1328–1427). On the capture of Pratāparudra II by the Emperor of Delhi, Vemā Reddi set up a kingdom with Addamki as capital. Yerranna, the last of the *Kavitraya* (the Great Three)[1] dedicated his *Harivaṁśa* to him. On his death, his eldest son, Anapota, and after him his second son, Anavema, succeeded to the kingdom, and changed the capital to Kondavīdu. Kumāragiri, son of Anapota, inherited from his uncle a kingdom which comprehended Palnādū and Veṅgī Nādū. He gave to his Prime Minister and brother-in-law, Kātayavema, the province of Rajahmundry, and made him the representative of the Reddi Dynasty in Veṅgī. After the death of Kumāragiri, a grandson of Māchā Reddi, brother of Vemā Reddi, usurped Kondavidu, and ruled as the lord of Palnādū. His son, Rācha Vema, was the last of this dynasty.

The Rajahmundry Branch. Kātayavema, the recipient of the province of Rajahmundry from Kumāragiri, and his son, also called Kumāragiri, had to defend their kingdom against the aggression of Komiti Vemā Reddi, the grandson of Māchā Reddi, and they were able to repel the aggressor through the able help and disinterested services of Allāda Reddi, who acted as the regent of Kumāragiri dur-

[1] See p. 42.

ing his minority. Kumāragiri was succeeded by his sister, Anatalli who married Vīrabhadra Reddi, son of Allāda Reddi. Pedda Kōmati Reddi, and his son, Rācha Vema, and Vīrabhadra Reddi of Rajahmundry, were all great scholars. Śrīnātha was the court poet attached to all these and he commemorates the dynasty in his *Palnādū Vīracharitra*, aptly called *Reddi Bhārata*. After 1427 the Reddi kingdom was absorbed into the kingdom of Vijayanagar.

2. **Padma Nayaks.** The officers of the army of the Kākatīya kings carved out petty kingdoms for themselves near Warangal. Of these, Sarvajña Siṁgama Bhūpāla was far-famed for his learning and literary attainments, which made him the terror of the poets. We find Śrīnātha, a poet of eminence, uttering a prayer for protection to Sarasvatī as he entered his council chamber. Bammera Pōtana, the author of the *Bhāgavata Purāṇa*, lived in his territory and was persecuted because he would not dedicate his *Bhāgavata* to him.

3. Of the three kingdoms which emerged out of the ruins of the Kākatīya Empire, that of **Vijayanagar** (A.D. 1327–1565) was destined to play an important rôle. It was called into existence by the imminent danger of annihilation with which the Hindu kingdoms were threatened by Muhammadan aggression. The first rumblings of the Muhammadan invasion were heard in the reign of Alla-ud-din Khilji, who sent an incursion into the country south of Narmada, which reached as far as Devagiri. The attack and fall of Warangal, and the captivity of Pratāparudra II, brought home to the Āndhras the meaning of the new menace. The establishment of the Bahmanī Kingdom, with its capital at Gulbarga, was a challenge which could no longer be neglected. The constant pressure, exerted by the invader across the border, united the Hindu kingdoms under the leadership of Vijayanagar, which attained its zenith under Kṛishṇadevarāya and kept the conqueror at bay for a good part of the century. The kingdom of Vijayanagar was founded by Harihara and Bukka Rāya with the assistance of their able minister, Vidyārañya Swāmi. The conflict with the Muhammadan powers went on with

varying fortunes, in the course of which Vijayanagar (1509–30) was more than once besieged and sacked. Kṛishṇadevarāya figures as the memorable king of the dynasty. The southern kingdoms submitted to his lordship, and he became the emperor of most of Southern India, from Veṅgī Nādū down to the modern Trichinopoly District. Kṛishṇadevarāya is known as Āndhra Bhoja, for his constant support and encouragement to Telugu literature. At his court there was a circle of eight poets, called the Ashṭa-Diggajās, who led a new literary movement known as the Prabandha movement. Kṛishṇadevarāya was succeeded by Achyuta Rāya, and in his reign the Hindu kingdom began to fall to pieces. After a few years of confusion, Rāma Rāya came to the throne. It was during his reign that a trio of great poets, Piṅgaḷī Sūranna, Rāmarāja Bhūshaṇa and Tenāli Rāmakṛishṇa existed. Rāma Rāya was defeated by the five kings of the Bahmanī kingdom in the battle of Tālikota, A.D. 1565, which marks the downfall of Vijayanagar's Empire. Kṛishṇadevarāya was a Vaishṇavite, and during his reign and that of his successor, the Vaishṇavism of Rāmānuja was practically the State religion, and a constant stream of Vaishṇava literature (corresponding to the Vīraśaiva literature of Kākatīya's reign) was kept up. Kṛishṇadevarāya wrote a prabandha called *Vishṇu Chittīya*, celebrating the saints and doctrines of Vaishṇavism.

The Bahmanī kings, on account of dissensions among themselves, were not able to take full advantage of their victory. Ultimately they were absorbed into the Moghul Empire, during the reign of Aurangzeb, in 1687. After the death of Aurangzeb in 1707, Nizam-ul-Mulk founded a hereditary dynasty, with Hyderabad as capital, which exercised a nominal authority over the entire south. The Carnatic was ruled by a deputy of the Nizam, the Nawab of the Carnatic. In the south, deputies of the Emperor of Vijayanagar declared their independence, and ruled their territories practically as their own. Thus Madura, Tanjore and Pudukkota became independent sovereign states. As in these three territories the deputies were Āndhras, we find, in the seventeenth and eighteenth centuries, considerable literary activity in Telugu. The literature of the period is known as the Southern School of Telugu literature.

The eighteenth century was marked by the wars between the French and the English. An event that has left a deep mark on the people and literature of the times is the struggle between the Marquis de Bussey, one of Dupleix's ablest subordinates, and the king of modern Vijayanagar in 1757. The story forms the subject-matter of Dittakavi Nārāyaṇa's *Rangarāya Charitra*, A.D. 1790, a popular version of which is still sung by troubadors all through the country. The issue of the struggle with the French was that the British power was finally established in South India. The Moghul Emperor, Shāh-Ālam, granted them the Dewani of Bengal, Behar, Orissa and the Northern Circars in 1764. In 1858, the Government of India was vested in the British Crown. The latter portion of the nineteenth and the beginning of the twentieth century are marked by the absorption of Western culture by the Āndhras, and the birth of the modern renaissance in Telugu literature.

The position of internal affairs, between the fall of the empire of Vijayanagar and the establishment of the British dominion, deserves notice, as it is with these conditions that Telugu literature is closely associated. The march and counter-march of the Muhammadan armies, the struggles of the French and the British, did not touch the Telugu poet so intimately as the rise and fall of minor principalities. During the rule of the Muhammadans and the British, the country was divided among Zamindars, some of whom were Reddis and others Padmanāyaks. These practically held their territory under the sovereigns of the day. Of these, the Rājas of Veṅkatagiri, Bobbili, Pithāpur and Vijayanagar deserve mention as the special patrons of literature from the seventeenth century up to the present time.

Religious Background. In order to follow the religious motive in Telugu literature, it is necessary to have a broad idea of the nature of the original faith of the Telugus, and the subsequent modifications which it underwent. The Supreme Being is regarded as having manifested in a Trinity of Power, Creation (*Sṛishṭi*), Maintenance (*Sthiti*) and Destruction (*Laya*), personified in

Brahmā, Vishṇu and Śiva. Of these, Brahmā has no temples and is not worshipped at all. The worship of Vishṇu and Śiva in their personal aspects may be said to constitute the basic elements in the faith of Hindus in general, and of the Telugus as participating in the general Hindu faith. The cults of Śiva and Vishṇu were carried on side by side, without any sense of conflict or animosity. It is on this background that the three movements, namely, those of Śaṅkara, Basava and Rāmānuja, began to operate. Śaṅkara's Advaitism, which had obtained general acceptance among Brāhmans, tended towards impersonalising both Siva and Vishṇu, and in consequence attenuating the personal element. It must, however, be said that on the Telugu mind Śaṅkara's philosophy produced rather a somewhat unexpected effect. It created a tendency towards eclecticism, in which Śiva and Vishṇu are regarded as equal, and equally worthy of worship. The Hari-Harā cult, which was expressly professed by some of the major poets of the first period, not only comprehended in its catholic outlook both Śiva and Vishṇu, but regarded the hyphenated deity as a necessary object of worship. In short, it attempted to combine two streams of religion which, till then, were flowing in separate and parallel lines. This cult held on for a time, but proved unsatisfactory to the old followers of either cult, and hence we soon find the Liṅgāyat movement on one side and the Rāmānuja movement on the other, exalting with renewed fervour Śiva and Vishṇu, each as an exclusive object of worship. Mādhvism, the third great religious movement, is a branch of Vaishṇavism, and exerts very little separately discernible influence. Islam—after the fall of Vijayanagar—and Christianity entered the country as religious influences in the eighteenth century, but exercised very little influence on literature.

III

THE LIFE OF A POET

THE poet in Telugu literature has played many a rôle in his time. In the twilight of society, he was the prophet specially endowed with powers of potent blessing and cursing. He was respected because he was feared. Bhīma Kavi curses Kaliṅga Gaṅgu, and he loses his throne. He blesses the widow of Potha Rājū with wedded happiness, and her dead husband comes back to life. When we next get a glimpse of the poet, we find he has shed much of his divinity, but has gained in dignity. He is a priest, learned in the *śāstras*, and versed in ritual. Kings rise from their seats to do him honour. Nanniah illustrates the type. The poet has scaled greater heights. He adorns the throne. Nannechōdu, Peddi Bhūpati, Kṛishṇadevarāya are royal poets whom a modern caricaturist would represent with pen in one hand and sword in the other. Descending a step, he may figure as a minister—the power behind the throne. Tikkanna heads the poets (of whom there are not a few) who have added the title 'Amātya' to their names. Śrīnātha was a courtier basking in royal sunshine. He was a pioneer of the peripatetic poets, who went from place to place, exhibiting skill and challenging rivals. They were of the order of knight-errants, who attended tournaments, engaged in combats—soldiers of fortune in the service of Sarasvatī. The poet attained to the zenith of his glory in the days of Kṛishṇadevarāya as the first citizen and foremost counsellor, honoured and respected by the king and the people. Peddana might well sit for a portrait of the happy poet. The seventeenth and eighteenth centuries mark the eclipse of the poet. Fallen from his high estate, he has taken refuge with petty

Poligars. Inspiration deserts him; he spins endless verses and holds the audience by literary acrobacy.

Kṛishṇadevarāya was a king after a poet's own heart. He delighted in the company of poets, and was never so happy as when a great poet came to his court. He enjoyed a good poem, honoured a true poet, made fun of the proud one when the mood was on him, and not infrequently himself entered the ring for a literary bout. The king's court was a royal academy, which weighed the poet in the balance and sent him forth with the imprimatur of approval. There, honour, riches, and above all true appreciation, awaited the poet. The informal durbars of the *literati* held by the emperor were the paradise of the poet.

The reward of the poet was honour, fame and the gratitude of his readers. He was not only immortal, but could confer immortality. Kings knew this well, and hence their attachment to him. Many a king lives in our memory because a great poet dedicated his poem to him; otherwise he would have been swept into oblivion. The poet did not disdain earthly honours. When a king sought the dedication of an epic or kāvya, he took care to pay the reward in advance, lest the poet's enthusiasm should wane. He gave him money, silk, musk, rubies, and gold ornaments. Occasionally, poets of first rank received largesses from the sovereign in the form of endowments. Sometimes the rewards took strange shapes. Śrīnātha speaks of the bath of gold he received in the court of Praudha Rāya. The poet was made to sit in the pearl-hall and *dīnars* and *taṅkas*—gold coins of the day—were poured over him. But more than money was the honour. It was a proud day for the poet when the king delighted to honour him. Kṛishṇadevarāya carried the palanquin of Peddanna, just to show his appreciation. It should not be supposed that all poets were rich, or that the poet had only to write a poem to be endowed with a village. No; by no means. Poverty was the normal badge of the Telugu poet. It is this touch of poverty that makes the world of poets akin. Ayyala Rājū Rāmabhadriah, unable to support his family, contemplated suicide. Śankuśāla Nṛisiṁha had to hawk his poems in the open street to pay his landlady. It was a strenuous life that the poet had to live. He had to undergo years of apprenticeship at his master's feet, then toil at his masterpiece, and finally effect an entry into the royal presence. This was by no means easy. Vested interests had to be propitiated and jealousies to be composed. His merit was his worst enemy. Atharvaṇa saw his lifework burnt to ashes by the jealousy of Nanniah. Śankuśāla Nṛisiṁha had to cool his heels in the corridors of the royal court and leave the place in disgust because Peddanna blocked his way. The poet's trouble did not end even with his entry into the coveted circle of royal poets. He had to be vigilant and maintain his position against rivals who challenged him and enemies who plotted against him. The Telugu poet, like his brethren all the world over, was a Bohemian and lived an unconventional life. Śrīnātha, Pinavīriah and Dhūrjatī were notorious for the riotous life they lived in their youth. They were a gay lot. They took the sweets and bitters of life as they came, and with the same serene composure feasted one day and starved the next. Śrīnātha in the stocks, Peddanna in tears, remind us of the tragic in the poet's life.

'Even great Homer nods at times.' Now and then we get a vivid glimpse of the poet's struggles. Tikkanna struggles for the right word, and his stenographer, a potter, comes to his aid. Potana wanders distraught for lack of a suitable phrase and finds his daughter has it before him. Pinavīranna stares at his palm leaves in despair. Tomorrow he has to read his *Bhārata* in the king's assembly, yet not a word is written. His lady-love saves him from dishonour and disgrace.

Romance, too, came in the poet's way. The queen, who has incurred the displeasure of her lord, seeks his mediation. Nandī Timmanna writes his *Parijātāpaharaṇa* to settle the imperial lovers' quarrel. Nṛisiṁha sells his stanzas in the street. The casement opens; the king's daughter enquires the price. 'A thousand a line,' cries the poet amazed. Money is paid on the spot. The starving poet goes back with money in his pocket, praise on his lips, and the image of the king's daughter in his heart.

The poet had his lighter moments too, when he delivered

his *obiter dicta*, in impromptu verse, on men and manners. He had his merry time, when he laughed with others and allowed others to laugh at him. He enjoyed a joke or a pun as much as any schoolboy. We see him poring over a 'limerick' (*samasya*) with the same devotion with which a modern reader wrestles with a crossword puzzle; and was there not among them a 'wag'—Tenāli Rāmakṛishṇa?

IV

LITERARY MODES AND FORMS

The Substance of the Literature. The substance of Telugu literature is preponderatingly religious. The epics, *Rāmāyaṇa*, *Mahābhārata*, *Bhāgavata*, and the *Purāṇas* are a vast storehouse of national culture from which the poets drew their material. The prodigious expenditure of time and talents which the translation of the epics involved led Śrīnātha to choose easily manageable portions of the epics for treatment. Episodes from the *Purāṇas*, under the name of Ākhyāna or Khāṇḍa, became popular. Of these the stories of *Nala* and *Harischandra* are easily the best favourities. From the sixteenth century onwards, the less known episodes from the *Purāṇas* are taken as the basis for kāvyas. Thus, the fortunes of a single hero under the title of Charitra, Vijaya, Vilāsa and Abhyudāya became a common subject-matter of poetry. In the eighteenth century, the canvas contracted still further and the marriage of heroes, under the designation of *Pariṇaya Kalyāṇa*, *Vivāha* became the order of the day. The avowedly religious literature consisted of biographies of the founders of religion, compendiums of religious teaching (*Sāra*), panegyrics of sacred places (*Mahātmya*), philosophical treatises and commentaries (*Bhāshya*); secular literature occupies a secondary place. The sciences, especially astrology, law, grammar, statecraft, archery fall under the latter head. Story and song, moral aphorisms, devotional psalms, are characteristic features of the popular literature. The drama is conspicuous by its absence. The Sanskrit Classics were also extensively translated. The lyric and the lampoon, though not regarded as separate departments, appear now and then.

The Literary Form. *Champu*, a mixture of prose and poetry, is all but universal as the vehicle of literary expression in verse. Tikkanna composed his *Uttara Rāmāyaṇa* completely in verse, eliminating prose altogether. Though this had some vogue, champu continued to be the dominant form. In translating epics from Sanskrit, it was found necessary, in order to avoid monotony, to use a variety of metres. This practice had also the advantage of allowing a variety of language to suit the variety of action. Varied metres are therefore the general rule. For popular literature, however, a single metre is generally chosen. *Dvipada* and *Śataka* are of this nature. Prose was a later discovery and did not come to its own till the eighteenth century A.D. But in the nineteenth and twentieth centuries the relative proportions of prose and poetry are reversed.

Authors' Craft. The highest form of composition in verse is *Praudha Prabandha* or *Mahā Kāvya.* The theory of poetics enunciates the essentials for such a composition as four in number: (1) *Śailī* (style), (2) *Pāka* (mould), (3) *Rasa* (sentiment), (4) *Alaṁkāra* (ornamentation).

Style. Style is either simple or 'praudha.' The latter involves an accumulation of phrases cemented together in a complex and difficult way. The words chosen are neither soft nor very musical, but dignified (Gambhira), sonorous, and majestic. Simple style had no attraction for the critics, and 'praudha,' with its complicated structure, was the standard aimed at. In style the Telugu writers generally hold up the qualities of *Mādhurya* (sweetness), *Sukumāra* (grace and delicacy), symphony, *Saurabhya* (fragrance) as worthy of attainment. In the choice of vocabulary, vulgar speech (*Grāmya*) is to be avoided.

Pāka (Mould). Equally important is pāka, or mould. There are three important pākas: *Drāksha* (wine), *Nārikeḷa* (coconut) and *Kadaḷi* (plantain). Pāka relates to the encasement of idea in language, and the nature and the texture of the language employed. Drāksha is crystal-clear style, where the idea is seen through the transparent medium. Nanniah employs this style. Kadaḷi is a little more difficult, the soft skin has to be peeled away before you reach the core. Tikkanna's style is an example of this mould. Nārikeḷa is the most difficult style and you have to break the hard rind to get at the idea. *Vishṇu Chittiyam* of Kṛishṇadevarāya is cast in this pāka.

Rasa, or sentiment, is the soul of poetry; the sūtra runs: "*Vākyam Rasathmakam Kāvyam.*" Of these rasas, there are nine: (1) *Śṛingāra* (love), (2) *Hāsya* (comic), (3) *Karuṇa* (pathos), (4) *Raudhra* (horror), (5) *Bhayānaka* (fear), (6) *Bībhatsa* (disgust), (7) *Vīra* (heroic), (8) *Adbhuta* (wonder), (9) *Sānta* (peace).

Though in a perfect kāvya there will be occasion to express all the nine rasas, in practice only a few of them are employed. In kāvya literature, as a matter of fact, śṛingāra (love) has crowded out all other rasas.

Alaṁkāra, or ornamentation. Great attention is paid by poets to alaṁkāra. There are *Śabdhālaṁkāras* (ornaments of sound), *Arthālaṁkāras* (ornaments of thought), *Slsha* (double entendre) and *Yamaka* (alliteration) are Śabdhālaṁkāras; *Upamāna* (simile) and *Utprekshā* (hyperbole) are figures of thought. In the construction of kāvya, descriptions occupy a central place. Cities, seas, mountains, seasons, sunrise, moonrise, water, sports, love passages, and weddings, all have to be described. In the kāvya, as it was developed by the Ashṭadiggajās of Rāya's court, the story is merely the framework upon which to hang these descriptions.

The General Form of Kavya. The poet begins with a short prayer containing the auspicious initial letter 'Śrī,' and invokes the blessing of God on his undertaking. The occasion or circumstances under which the work is undertaken (usually the royal command) is next stated. Tikkanna mentions the appearance of his favourite deity in a dream, suggesting the dedication of *Bhārata* to himself. This is copied by later poets, who fondly imagine that their effusions interest both gods and men. Poets have dedicated their poems either to patrons or deities; the latter are considered to be superior to the former. Then follows a description of the lineage and achievements of the patron and his ancestors, of the poet and his ancestors. From the time of Nannechodu (though it is supposed that Tikkanna set the fashion), the practice of adding *Sastyantamulu*

—a stanza in which each word or phrase ends with the preposition 'to'—grew up. The story then begins, and is related continuously. The subject matter is generally Purāṇic. A slender Purāṇic basis, which admits room for imagination, is preferred to pure invention. Piṅgaḷi Sūranna is the first poet to take a purely invented story for his theme. Some poets add the praise of good poets and the condemnation of the bad. This gives them an opportunity to dilate upon their views of poetic composition. It is usual to bow to the *Kavitraya* before beginning the composition. The story is divided into cantos, at the end of each of which there is a short subscription containing a formal statement that such and such a poet has written the prabandha.

V

EARLY BEGINNINGS, THE DESI AND THE MARGI

At the outset of Telugu literature, we are confronted with a problem which does not at present admit of a final solution. The earliest literary work of which we can be certain is Nanniah's translation of the first three cantos of the *Mahābhārata* in A.D. 1020. Nanniah's *Bhārata* is a classic of the highest order. It is against all principles of literary evolution that a 'classic,' so sublime in its conception, and so faultless in composition, should have emerged without antecedent stages of development. So the theory is urged, with much cogency and force, that there must have existed much pre-Nanniah literature, probably Jain in authorship, which was destroyed by those who were responsible for the Brahminical reaction known as the Vaidikī movement. This theory, towards which the modern mind, imbued with notions of growth and continuity in literature, naturally inclines, is, however, beset with difficulties. The case against it may be stated thus: The researches of well-nigh a quarter of a century, in the course of which hundreds of Telugu books have been recovered from oblivion, have not produced a single work for which an earlier date than Nanniah can be assigned. Nannechodu's *Kumāra Sambhava* is now regarded by an increasing number of competent critics as post-Nanniah. Nor have the labours of epigraphists and palæologists brought to light any Telugu inscription earlier than A.D. 1020. In further confirmation of this fact is the persistent tradition that Nanniah is the pioneer of Telugu literature and the legislator of the Telugu language, '*Vagānu Śāsana.*' It is very significant that tradition does not retain the memory of any earlier poet. The argument that the earlier Jain literature was destroyed by Brahminical jealousy lacks historical confirmation; and, even if true, it is insufficient to explain the extinction of an extensive literature without leaving any traces behind. In the Tamil country, where the conflict between Jainism and Śaivism has been far more intensive, we find that Jain literature has survived all attempts at deliberate destruction. Moreover, fanaticism may account for the destruction of books, but not for the effacement of the memory of poets. The evidence against this theory is not merely negative. We have the positive testimony of Ketana that there was no Telugu grammar prior to his. Further, a study of the poetry of the period between Nanniah and Tikkanna leaves the impression that the poets were mastering, with various degrees of success, a regulative science recently inaugurated. Of lesser probative value are the following facts: (1) that Telugu scholars, before the eleventh century, used to go to the Kanarese country and write in Kanarese; and (2) that the earliest existing grammars are in Sanskrit, which are hardly to be expected if there was in existence any literature in Telugu. To crown all, there is reasonable probability that the Telugu script in the current form took shape in about the eleventh century A.D. Weighty as these considerations are, we are not driven to choose between a state of facts against all canons of literary evolution and a theory for which no verification is possible. A clue to a mediatory theory is afforded by the existence in Telugu literature of two streams; an earlier one called *Deśī*, and a later one called *Mārgī*. The indigenous Deśī type exists mostly in song and sonnets and is independent of Sanskrit. It is essentially a rural literature unsuited for elaborate forms of composition. The religious revival of the eleventh century A.D. necessitated the translation of the major epics from Sanskrit for which the resources of the Deśī type of literature were inadequate. An artificial system had to be manufactured to meet the new contingency. A new grammar, a new prosody and a new rhetoric, mostly borrowed from or fashioned after the Sanskrit model, had to be forged. It was the Telugu-Sanskrit scholars who were expected to lead the new movement, and this explains why the early grammars were in Sanskrit. The Sanskrit-Telugu literature is thus pre-eminently an artificial system, and hence has neither growth nor continuity. There is no natural transition from the epic to the kāvya. Living things, like trees, have origin and growth, a beginning and an end. Artificial structures, like pyramids, do not grow but are built. In translating from a foreign literature, the elaborate may precede the simple, an epic may be translated before a sonnet. There is nothing unnatural in the artificial system having its origin in Nanniah, or a few decades earlier. This does not exclude the existence of *any* pre-Nanniah literature, but only the existence of Telugu-Sanskrit literature before Nanniah. We may, on the basis of the foregoing conclusions, formulate tentatively the following propositions:

1. That here was originally a literature called Deśī, indigenous, and having affinity with the Dravidian rather than the Aryan literature. The bulk of pre-Nanniah literature was of this type.

2. That Nanniah was one of the earliest representatives, if not the founder, of the Mārgī literature, which dates from the eleventh century. It is unlikely that we shall be able to trace Telugu-Sanskrit literature further up than the middle of the tenth century. The earlier attempts are represented by the two *śāsanas*, (inscriptions) of *Yuddha Malla*, and *Mopur*.

3. That the two currents have run parallel in Telugu literature.

4. That the growing influence of Sanskrit-Telugu literature diverted literary efforts to itself, and grew in volume and range, imposing its prosody and rhetoric on Desi literature.

The Pre-Nanniah Literature. The Deśī, as already pointed out, is the native literature of the Telugus. It lets us into the world of thoughts and ideas of the unsophisticated Telugu mind. In form and context, the Deśī stands in clear contrast to the Mārgī literature. The latter is essentially court-poetry—artificial and complicated in structure, and elaborate in technique. The former is fundamentally rural in outlook, simple in its structure and sentiment, and natural and graceful in expression. The verse rarely exceeded seven or eight lines; the metre is built on a syllabic basis and not on *mātra* or tone values of Sanskrit prosody; *Yati* and *Prasa*[1] are observed, in common with other Dravidian languages. Vemana's quartets and dvipada, from which Nanniah in all probability composed his *Taruvoja*, *Akkaras* and *Sīsam* represent the higher reaches of Deśī metrical art. It consisted of song, sonnet and story, and never rose to the complexity of a kāvya or epic. It may be characterised as the poetry of the simple mind in vital touch with nature, expressing itself in sharp, brisk lines touched with colour and animation.

What did it deal with? It dealt mostly with the domestic life of the cottage and the communal life of the village. Kings, palaces and wars were beyond its range. The maids at the well, the mother at the cradle, the lovers in the moonlight, the labourer in the field, and the local hero of the tribal wars were some of its themes. We may classify this literature under the following heads:

1. Songs of the Cradle (*Lāli-Pāṭalu*).
2. Songs of the Dawn (*Melu Kolupulu*).
3. Songs of Festivity (*Mangaḷa Hāratulu*).
4. Songs of Love (*Zavaḷīlu*).
5. Songs of Devotion (*Kirtanas*).
6. Songs of the Harvest (*Ūdupu Pāṭalu*).
7. Songs of the Teamster (*Kūli Pāṭalu*).
8. Songs of Wine (*Kaḷḷu Pāṭalu*).
9. Songs of Play (*Āta Pāṭalu*).
10. Proverbs (*Samitelu*).
11. Stories (*Kathalu*).
12. Sagas of Local Chiefs (Ballads).

In these we have Telugu poetry in its purest strain—not the hybrid Sanskrit collations of post-Nanniah literature. This is a literature racy of the soil, and full of lyrics of intense realism and concentrated power.

[1] The central and the vertical rhymes.

VI

PURANA YUGA, OR THE AGE OF TRANSLATION

The first stage in the development of Telugu literature—a period covering five centuries—is marked by the introduction and extension of Sanskrit culture, mainly through translations. The impulse for translation had its origin in the revival of Brahminism and the zeal to spread the Vaidikī movement, which it originated. This religious movement had the support of the kings, the approbation of the *literati*, and above all the sympathy of the people. The long-drawn struggle between Jainism and Hinduism had ended in the victory of Brahminism and the triumph of the worship of Śiva in the Tamil and Kanarese countries. That this triumph of Hinduism spread its contagious spiritual impetus to the Āndhra-land hardly admits of doubt. The victory of Hinduism, now assured beyond dispute by the decay of Jainism, had to be consolidated and the hearts of the people rendered immune to the possible renewal of assaults by the vanquished faiths. The opening of the flood-gates of Sanskrit culture was the final act of insurance against relapse in the future. This explains why, in Telugu literature, translations mark the initial, and not, as in other Dravidian vernaculars, the later, stage. This also accounts for the preponderatingly religious character and the extensive range of the translations.

The Aryan religion in its popular and non-philosophical form is embodied in three classics: the *Mahābhārata*, known as the 'fifth Veda'[1]; the *Rāmāyaṇa*, the story of Rāma; and the *Bhāgavata Purāṇa*, the story of Kṛishṇa.

[1] Often referred to simply as the *Bhārata*.

The solid achievement of this period is the translation of all these three epics into Telugu.

The Translation of the Mahabharata. This colossal undertaking, rendered all the more onerous and sacred by the circumstances which made the translation necessary, took three centuries to accomplish. It was begun by Nanniah in the eleventh century A.D., continued by Tikkanna in the thirteenth century A.D., and concluded by Errāpragada in the fourteenth. A grateful posterity enthroned them together in its memory and crowned them with the title 'Kavitraya'—the Great Three. No subsequent poet, down to our times, ever attempted to invoke the muse without paying his tribute to the three great masters.

Nanniah (Title, 'Vagānu Śāsana').—Nanniah, who began the translation of the *Mahābhārata* at the command of the Chāḷukyā king, Rāja-Rāja-Narendra (1022–63), was a Vaidikī Brahmin of Mugdala Gotra, from Tanuku, in Veṅgī Nādū. He was the family *purohit* or priest of the reigning monarch, and had a reputation for great piety and scholarship in Sanskrit. He relates, in the prologue, the circumstances under which his royal master desired him to translate the epic. Rāja-Rāja-Narendra, like many monarchs of his day, claimed to be a descendant of the lunar kings, whose progenitors, the Pāṇḍavas, are celebrated in the *Mahābhārata*. He was fond of hearing the epic and emulating its heroes. Having heard the story in many languages, probably in Tamil and Kanarese, he was desirous to perpetuate it in the language of the country of which he was the ruler. There was no man of his day better qualified, by his learning and piety, for this task than Nanniah; so it was entrusted to him. He composed the Ādi and Sabhā cantos, and a portion of the Araṇya Parva. Various stories are told to account for the non-completion of this canto. One story is that Atharvaṇa wrote a *Bhārata* and showed it to Nanniah before he took it to the king. Nanniah, fearing that, if Atharvaṇa's superior composition reached the king, his own might not be accepted, set fire to the house in which Atharvaṇa's manuscript was deposited. Atharvaṇa, seeing his labour of years reduced to ashes, cursed Nanniah and he became mad. But as Nanniah and Atharvaṇa were not contemporaries the story is not worthy of credence. There is also the fact that stanzas from Atharvaṇa's *Bhārata* are given in later anthologies. Five other books are attributed to Nanniah, namely: (1) *Āndhra Śabda Chintāmaṇi*, otherwise known as *Prakriyākaumudī*; (2) *Lakshaṇa Sāra*; (3) *Indra Vijaya*; (4) *Chāmundī Vilāsa*; and (5) *Rāghavābhyudaya*. But, in all probability, none of these were written by him. As Chāmundī was the titular deity of the Chāḷukyās, it is possible that he wrote *Chāmundī Vilāsa*; but the existing work differs so much in style from Nanniah's that we may well doubt his authorship of it.

Nanniah's style is in Drāksha Pāka,[1] simple, sweet and graceful. Language delicately responds to emotion and gracefully adjusts itself to the changing action of the story, and to the varying moods of the actors. The poet employs a variety of metres suitable to the wide range of passions and events so characteristic of the epic. Though a translation, the Telugu *Bhārata* is really an independent work of art, superior to the original in many respects. Nanniah wrote the *Bhārata* in 'Champū.'[2] His prose is of two varieties, one simple and the other more complicated, but always less artificial and cumbrous than the stilted stateliness of kāvya prose. In his vocabulary, he employs two-thirds Sanskrit and one-third Telugu words. Jakkanna, a later poet, characterises his poetry as '*Rasabandhura Bhāvābhi Rāmamu*'—'beautiful ideas in bright emotional setting.' Nanniah began his epic with a Sanskrit sloka of praise. His example was copied by Raṅganātha and others, till Tikkanna set a new fashion.

Narayana Bhat. A contemporary of Nanniah, Nārāyaṇa Bhaṭ deserves mention, if for no other reason than for the praise which he has received from Nanniah. He says, 'Just as Kṛishṇa assisted Arjuna in the great war, Nārāyaṇa Bhaṭ helped me in my labours.' It is not clear what exactly were the nature of the services which Nārāyaṇa Bhaṭ ren-

[1] See above p. 34. [2] Ibid.

dered to Nanniah. It is suggested that he really composed the major portion of the *Bhārata*, now wrongly attributed to Nanniah. This is unlikely, because if Nārāyaṇa Bhaṭ had been a poet of equal eminence with Nanniah he would have continued the translation of the *Bhārata*; unless it be that he pre-deceased Nanniah ,for which we have no evidence. Nor do the first three cantos manifest any signs of a joint composition. It is more likely that Nārāyaṇa Bhaṭ helped Nanniah in his efforts to inaugurate the Vaidikī movement, as Śrī Kṛishṇa helped Arjuna to establish *Dharma*. It is possible also that Nanniah was engaged in a conflict with the Jains on the one hand and the orthodox reactionaries,who opposed the translation of sacred literature, on the other. Though no work of his has survived, Nārāyaṇa Bhaṭ was evidently a poet of eminence. He was well versed, as stated in the Nandimapūdi inscription, in Sanskrit, Karṇāṭaka, Prākṛit, Paiśāchika. As a reward for his learning the emperor made him the gift of the village of Nandimapūdi. He is said to have defeated many a proud poet and earned the title *Kavibhāva Vajrāṅkuśa* (The Terror of Rival Poets).

Tikkanna Yagvi (A.D. 1220–1300. Title 'Kavi Brahma'). For nearly two centuries the *Bhārata* was where Nanniah left it, till a great poet, worthy to continue it, came into the literary world in the person of Tikkanna. The reasons for the long delay in the emergence of a competent poet were many. There was a school of obscurantists who regarded the translation and the consequent publication of *Bhārata* to the world as sinful, especially because it was regarded as the fifth Veda, the reading and hearing of which is prohibited to non-Brahmins. The madness which befell Nanniah, who set at naught this theological injunction, strengthened the superstition that those who touch the *Araṇya Parva* would come to grief. But, above all these fears, there was the natural reluctance on the part of poets to challenge comparison with Nanniah by continuing his work. Nanniah was a poet much in advance of his age, and the art of composition which he evolved was a science which few had yet mastered. It was, therefore, natural that, in spite of the efforts of rulers, few ventured to come forward to undertake the task. Tradition, which regards Nanniah and Tikkanna as contemporaries, has an interesting story to relate, which, though not of any historical value, throws much light on the difficulties which the rulers, with all their wealth and influence, had to face in inducing competent poets to continue the translation of the *Bhārata.*

With a view to discover whether a poet of Nanniah's eminence would be forthcoming, Rāja-Rāja-Narendra caused to be circulated a stanza, considered to be Nanniah's best, throughout his realm, with a request that other poets should compose a similar stanza embodying the same idea. Various attempts were made, but all of them were rejected by the king's council of pandits as below the mark. But there was one poet who simply copied the stanza and coloured it red and sent it to the king. The council construed the act of the poet as an announcement that he could not only compose like Nanniah, but even excel him, by adding a new lustre to his composition. Enquiries showed that the poet's was no empty boast and that his learning was equal to the task set to him. The emperor commanded the feudatory chief, in whose jurisdiction the poet lived, to send him to the imperial presence. The order was sooner given than obeyed; for the poet refused to leave his native place, in spite of persuasion and promise of tempting rewards. The chieftain, vexed at the obduracy of the poet, threatened him with punishment, and swore that if he did not go to the emperor, he would have him shaved, led through the street in procession on a donkey, would make him live outside the city in a hut, and disgrace him by forcing him to eat flesh. Threats proved as unavailing as promises of gifts. The emperor, anxious that the translation of the *Bhārata* should begin at once, was willing to allow him to remain in his native place if only he would commence the work. The local chief was placed in a dilemma by the condescension of the emperor, between keeping to his threats and reconciling himself to the poet. The expedient he struck upon was to request the poet to perform *Yajña*—a purificatory sacrifice, in the course of which, according to the prescribed ritual, he had to shave himself, live outside the city and eat flesh. The poet who caused so much embarrassment to his chieftain was none other than Tikkanna.

Tikkanna was a Niyogī Brahmin attached to the court of Manumasiddhi, the ruler of Nellore, a tributary chief under the Kākatīya king, Gaṇapati Deva. He came from a family illustrious in the annals of the district, as having given to the country warriors of renown and poets of repute. The Kottaruvu family, to which the poet belonged, came originally from Vellatūru in the Kṛishṇa District, and settled in Guntur. His grandfather, Bhāskara, was a poet of eminence and is reputed to have written a Telugu *Rāmāyaṇa* which is lost. His father, Kommanna, was the head of the army of the local chief in Guntur. His 'second cousin,' Khadga Tikkanna, or 'Tikkanna of the Sword,' more than once saved his master by his valour on the battlefield. Tikkana, on account of his family influence, was more of a minister than a mere poet, honoured by his master and treated by him as his equal. On one occasion, when his master was driven out of his country by his relatives, Akkana and Bayyana, Tikkanna was entrusted with the mission of securing for him the good offices of Kākatīya Gaṇapati; and it was to Tikkanna that Manuma owed his reinstatement.

Before Tikkanna began the translation of the *Bhārata* he composed *Nirvachanottara Rāmāyaṇa*, an all-verse composition relating the story of Rāma after his coronation, and describing his reign, his conquests and his death. It will be remembered that Nanniah wrote in Champu. Tikkanna seems to have thought the all-verse composition very difficult of attainment. For some reason or other he did not finish the last canto, but Jayantī Rāmabhut completed it later on. It is said that Tikkanna was the author of *Vijaya Sena*, and a treatise on prosody called *Kavi-Vākbandhana*, but of this we cannot be sure, as these works are not available.

The poet's title to fame rests on his translation of the *Bhārata*. Afraid of beginning where Nanniah had left the story, that is, from the middle of the *Aranya Parva*, lest some evil should befall him, Tikkanna commenced with the *Virāta Parva*, and finished the remaining fifteen cantos.

Many interesting stories are told to illustrate his extraordinary learning and unfailing inspiration. He undertook to dictate his verses in open court, without referring to the Sanskrit original, and made a vow that if ever he hesitated for a word he would cut off his tongue. Tikkanna composed so quickly that it was difficult to get anyone who could take down what he delivered, till at last a competent amanuensis was found, at the suggestion of the poet himself, in one Kumāra Gurunātha, a potter by caste, who was not only an expert stenographer, but a pandit of some attainment, as the sequel showed. It was under these interesting conditions that the translation proceeded, much to the wonder of the pandits, who were astonished at the unbroken flow of verse. Once, and once only, did Tikkanna hesitate for the right word, and as the right word did not come he gave up the effort and exclaimed, 'What shall I say, Gurunātha?' The poet was disconsolate; but the amanuensis was equal to the occasion and finished the stanza with the very words which Tikkanna uttered in despair, and which, by a strange coincidence, exactly fitted the context, as an exclamation to the Kurunātha (Lord of Kurus). When this was pointed out, Tikkanna's joy knew no bounds, and he was all praise for the potter. This story, though probably apocryphal, illustrates the popular estimate of the poet's incomparable versatility. Another story, related in this connection, is that the pandits of the court, who observed that Tikkanna used common metres and simple style, began to murmur that he knew no better. Indignant at this insult, he composed *Sauptika*, and *Strī Parvas* in such difficult metres and Sanskrit compounds that it was beyond the comprehension of his erstwhile critics, who, chastened, implored him to return to his original style.

Tikkanna, in his prologue, shows considerable originality, and gave currency to certain conventions which were copied by others. He began with a condemnation of incompetent poets and a praise of the competent ones. This was necessitated by the literary conditions of the day, when many poets sought recognition who paid little attention to technique and composition. The second feature is the introductory dream, in which his grandfather appeared and delivered him a message from Harihara Nātha, that he should dedicate the *Bhārata* to him. The third is a hymn of praise, with every word ending in the possessive case (*sastyantamulu*). Later poets have mechanically copied these features.

The qualities of style which procured Tikkanna the title of 'Kavi Brahma' are twofold. The first is his conciseness of diction. He always studied economy in the use of words. It is difficult to alter a single word of his compact phrases without seriously impairing their value and richness of meaning. He was a very conscientious stylist and spared no pains in refining his verse. The second quality is his realism. Unlike the Prabandha poets, whose 'characters' move like puppets cleverly manipulated, Tikkanna inspires his heroes with life. At his touch the past springs up into life. The dead cities awake once more and the streets throng with busy crowds. Ancient palaces become alive with kings, courtiers and courtesans. The famous battle-fields echo to the tread of warriors, the rumbling of chariots and the cries of combatants. The poet attained the height of his art in *Virāta Parva*.

Errapragada (A.D. 1280–1350. Title, 'Śambhudāsa' or 'Prabandha Parameśvāra'). Fifty years after Tikkanna, Errāpragada completed the portion of the *Araṇya Parva* still remaining unfinished. So potent was the belief that the poet who touches this Parva would come to grief, that Śambhudāsa made it appear that it was Nanniah who completed it, by dedicating it to Rāja-Rāja-Narendra. Errāpragada was a Niyogī from Gudlūru in Kandukur Taluk, Nellore District, and was attached to Proliah Vemā Reddy, the ruler of the district. He says in *Harivaṁśa*—his second work—that his father, Śrī Sūrya, was a poet in two languages and a *yogī* who became a *siddha*. He relates how Tikkanna appeared to him in a dream and encouraged him to complete the *Bhārata*. Not satisfied with his contribution to the *Bhārata*, he began *Harivaṁśa*, which is in the nature of an epilogue to the *Bhārata*, and traces the fortunes of the heroes of the epic after the fateful war. Other poems attributed to him are, *Rāmāyaṇa*, *Lakshmī Nṛtsiṁha Purāṇa*, known also as *Ahobala Mahātmya*.

Errāpragada is a staunch Śaivite, a disciple of a yogī, Śaṅkaraswāmī. In points of literary merit he is worthy of being ranked with Nanniah and Tikkanna. His ability as a poet is manifest from the fact that he begins his work in the style of Nanniah and, imperceptibly, passes into that of Tikkanna. He was able to simulate them so well that the reader does not, till he is told, realise that between Nanniah and Tikkanna a third poet had intervened. His control of language and his variety of style are remarkable. His style is more difficult than that of Nanniah and Tikkanna. He writes in Kadaḷi Pāka.[1] His devotion has earned him the title of 'Śaṁbhudāsa' (Servant of Śiva), and his command of versification the title of 'Prabandha Parameśvara' (Lord of the Verse). Śrīnātha admires his felicitous combination of phrases (*Sūkti Vaichitrī*). He uses Sanskrit and Telugu words in equal proportions.

Bharata Translators. In order to complete the story of the translation of the *Bhārata* we have had to anticipate two centuries. We will now return to the chronological order. Before doing so, we may make a few general remarks about other translators of the *Bhārata*, which, like its sister epic, the *Rāmāyaṇa*, has been variously interpreted. The Brahminical version, which is also the widely accepted and popular one, regards the hero, Kṛishṇa, as a divine incarnation, and the whole story as having the sanctity of a supplementary Veda. The Jains, who renounced the theological system of the Brahmins, gave currency to a version in which all the heroes are regarded as merely *Kāraṇa Purushas*—men of destiny—sent into this world to fulfil a special mission. It is probable that Atharvaṇa's *Bhārata*, which Nanniah is said to have suppressed, is a Jaina *Bhārata*; and it is all the more likely that it was so, as the author was a Jain by faith. Jaiminī gave a slightly different version of the story, known as *Jaiminī Bhārata*, which only deals with the portion of *Bhārata* relating to the *Aśvamedha Yāja* of Yudhishṭhira, and differs in many details from the

[1] See above p. 34.

Sanskrit original. This has been translated by Pillala Marri Pinavīra Bhadriah in the fifteenth century A.D. The epic is continued under the name of *Harivaṁśa*, which relates the fortunes of Kṛishṇa after the war. Errāpragada translated it into Telugu, and Nāchana Soma versified a portion of the story, under the name *Uttara Harivaṁśa*, in 1380. There are any number of prose versions of the story written by recent authors.

Eleventh Century Poets. The eleventh and twelfth centuries are *terra incognita* in Telugu literary history. The literature of the time is being slowly recovered by the indefatigable energy of research scholars. We are sure, from the references in subsequent poems, that these centuries must have been most fertile, and yet tradition has transmitted to us the names and works of only a few of the poets. The dominant poet of the eleventh century is (as we have said) Nanniah, whose translation of the *Bhārata* inaugurates the era of translations. There is only one other poet, who, though not his contemporary, yet belongs to his century, and his name is Pāvalūri Mallanna (1060–70), a Niyogī Brahmin and the *karṅam* (accountant) of the village Pavalūr, near Guntur in Kamma Nādū. He translated into verse a mathematical treatise of Mahāvīr-āchāryalu in Sanskrit. The author follows Nanniah's example of placing a Sanskrit śloka at the beginning of his book—an example not generally followed by the poets after him. Though the Sūtras are taken from the Sanskrit original, the mathematical calculations are his own. In Sanskrit literature the names of Brahmagupta, Vīrachārya, Bhāskārāchārya and Jagannātha stand out as eminent mathematicians. Of these, Vīrachārya's treatise has been translated into Telugu by Mallana, and into Kanarese by Rājāditya in the same century. Eluganṭi Peddanna translated *Līlāvatī* by Bhāskārāchārya under the name of *Prakīrṇa Gaṇiṭa*. There is a *Sūtra Gaṇita*, composed, during the reign of Pratāparudra, by an unknown author.

Mahāvīrāchārya's book contains chapters on mensuration, the measurement of shadows, proper and mixed fractions and the theory of numbers. It is natural that the author, who was a karṅam, should turn his attention to mathematics. It is said that he also wrote *Bhadrādri Rāmaśataka*. This is doubtful; for, though the names of the authors are the same, the names of their fathers differ.

Twelfth Century Poets. The twelfth is a century of royal poets and state religions. The dominant note of the century is the intensification of the religious consciousness of the people and the consequent birth of aggressive and propagandist creeds which sought the aid of kings for their expansion. Rāmānuja began his missionary tours about the middle of this century. The Vīravaishṇava faith gave rise to the Vīraśaiva faith associated with Basava. Religions ran into extremes. It is in this century that Telugu literature began to be influenced by Liṅgāyatism. The three poets of this period are all supporters and propagandists of this faith.

1. **Prataparudra I** (A.D. 1140–96) was a Kākatīya prince who made his reign illustrious by extensive conquests. He was a Vīraśaiva by faith and used his power for the spread of his religion by giving largesses to propagandists, poets and preachers. He is the author of *Nīti Sāra* in Sanskrit and in Telugu. It is natural and appropriate that a king should write on king-craft. In Sanskrit there is an extensive literature on Political Ethics, of which *Śukranīti*, *Pañchatantra* and *Chāṇakya Nītisāra* are the outstanding examples. It does not appear whether this treatise is a translation or an original composition. In the next century Beddana, another king, wrote a book on the same subject, and refers to Pratāparudra as his predecessor in the line.

2. **Palakuriki Somanatha,** a Liṅgāyat propagandist, flourished in his reign. Somanātha was a prolific writer on Śaivism. He composed his poems in three languages: Telugu, Kanarese and Sanskrit. Through books and pamphlets, polemics and disputations, he carried a missionary campaign which had the support of the court. Of his Telugu books, *Paṇḍitārādhya Charita*, *Dvipada Basava Purāṇa* and *Anubhava Sāra* may be mentioned.

The first of these books was utilised by Śrīnātha for his work of the same name. Piduparti Somanātha composed the *Basava Purāṇa* in verse some time later (1510). Somanātha had for his disciple the minister of Pratāparudra, Nindutūri Yannayāmātya.

3. **Nannechodu.** (A.D. 1150– . Title, 'Kavi Rāja Śikhāmaṇi,' 'Tenkaṇamātya') was an Āndhra Choda of Pākanādū. He was the author of *Kumāra Sambhava*, a Mahākāvya. He is also said to have composed another book called *Kaḷāvilāsa*, which, however, is lost. In the prologue of his *Kumāra Sambhava* he states he is the son of Chodaballi, Lord of Pākanādū, and describes the capital of his kingdom as Orayūr on the Kāveri, in the Trichy District, in which place we are told in all seriousness that stone trees blossom and stone cocks crow! It cannot be maintained that Orayūr was really the capital. As the family originally came from Kāveri, the convention was cherished, in defiance of geography, that their ancient family abode was the capital of the Telugu dominion.

The *Kumāra Sambhava* is a recent discovery, unearthed by the industry of Mr. M. Rāmakṛishṇa, M.A., who claims that the poet belongs to the tenth century A.D.—a claim not confirmed by critical examination. It is dedicated to Jaṁgama Mallikārjuna, a Liṅgāyat of renown. *Kumāra Sambhava* ranks high in the literature of the day. In Sanskrit, Kālidāsa and Udbhaṭa had written on the subject. Our poet has not followed either the one or the other exclusively, but has taken them both as his basis. Certain characteristic features of the poem are noticeable. Nannechodu is the first poet to employ Kanarese and Tamil words in Telugu poems. Though this practice is not objectionable in itself, and is even commendable where it adds to the beauty of verse, the poet cannot be said to have been discreet in the use of foreign words. His style, too, is not faultless. *Sandhis* not approved by standard grammarians are used by him. Notwithstanding these minor faults, there can be hardly any doubt of his extensive and massive learning in Sanskrit and Kanarese. In his composition he shows a perceptible partiality to Kanarese metres. Atharvaṇa, the grammarian, has instanced him as one who courted death by using inauspicious metres. It would appear that he had no knowledge of auspicious and inauspicious *gaṇas* and, as a result, employed metres which proved calamitous in the end. He began his poem with *sragdharā*, in which, according to the rules of prosody, he had to use *magaṇa* followed by *ragaṇa*,[1] which is inauspicious. Nannechodu lost his life shortly after in the internecine wars of the period. Another interesting fact is that Nannechodu used in his prologue the praise of good poets and *sastyantamulu*.[2] Posterity associated these features with Tikkanna. But Nannechodu robs Tikkanna of his laurels in this respect.

Thirteenth Century Poets. Raṅganātha and Bhāskara, one at the beginning and the other at the end of the thirteenth century, remind us that this was pre-eminently a century of *Rāmāyaṇa* translators. Tikkanna continued the translation of *Bhārata*. We need hardly say that the age of Rāma's worship is the age of Vaishṇavism as well. The story of Rāma, in its popular and literary appeal, excels the sister epic, the *Mahābhārata*. While we have in Telugu literature only one translation of the *Mahābhārata*, which took three centuries for completion, there is a surfeit of renderings of the *Rāmāyaṇa*. From the time of Nanniah, down to V. Subbā Rao in the twentieth century, there is hardly a century which did not witness several attempts at the translation of this epic. As for the incidents and episodes of the *Rāmāyaṇa*, the literary efforts they have called forth are innumerable.

Vālmīki's classic has always been the basis of these translations. Vālmīki was not only a historian of Rāma, but a champion of Aryan culture and Hinduism, and naturally his version, with all its theological implications, has been accepted by Hindus all over India. The Jains, who had renounced Brahmin theology, had their own version of the *Rāmāyaṇa*, wherein, as in the case of the Jain *Bhārata*,

[1] In verse the prosodical unit is a gaṇa—so many gaṇas of so much tone value making a line. A gaṇa is made up of the prescribed sound elements, the short ones being called *laghus*, the long ones *dīrghas*.

[2] See pp. 35 f., 48.

the hero and the heroine are represented not as incarnations of God, but as persons of destiny, and the mythological and miraculous elements are more or less excluded. The Jain version is not represented in Telugu. The story of Rāma after the recovery of Sītā, relating to his reign, the birth of his children and his death, forms as it were an epilogue to the epic, and is known as *Uttara Rāmāyaṇa.* This has been translated, as we have already indicated, by Tikkanna in all-verse, and by Kāchavibhudu in Dvipada, and by Kāṁkanti Pāparāju in Champu. The story has been allegorised and spiritualised under the names of *Adhyātma* and *Vasishṭha Rāmāyaṇa.* The characters of the story are regarded as symbolising the various incidents in the 'Pilgrim's Progress of the Soul'; Rāma as God, Sīta as the individual soul, Rāvaṇa as *Māyā.* Madiki Siṁganna, in the fifteenth century, translated the *Vāsishṭa Rāmāyaṇa.* Kaṇāda Peddana Somayājī composed the *Adhyātma Rāmāyaṇa* of Viśvamitra in verse in 1750. Another school of thought, which conceived of life in cycles, in each of which the main events are reproduced in a more or less reduced form, maintained that the *Rāmāyaṇa* was enacted in various *yugas—dvāpara*, *tretā*, and *kāli*; and has assayed to give the story as it happened in a previous yuga. One of such versions is represented in Telugu by the *Śatakanṭa Rāmāyaṇa*, attributed to Bhīma Kavi. In the thirteenth century we have two translations, one in two-feet metre by Raṅganātha, and the other in Champu by Bhāskara. In Kṛishṇadevarāya's time a lady, belonging to the potter caste, Molla by name, composed the *Rāmāyaṇa* in verse. In the seventeenth and eighteenth centuries, literal prose translations began to appear. Then we have a translation in pure Telugu by Kūchimanchi Timmanna Kavi, and translations adapted to the stage and set to music. Without being a literal translation, the story of Rāma is told under the name of *Rāghavābhyudaya* by Nanniah, and Ayyala Rāzu Rāmabhadriah. There is no epic which has been so often or so variously translated as the *Rāmāyaṇa.*

1. **Ranganatha** (A.D. 1230–40). The century opens with a translation in couplets of *Rāmāyaṇa* by Raṅganātha.

Though associated with the name of Raṅganātha, it was really composed, as the internal evidence and the explicit reference in the *Colophon* show, by Buddha Rāzu, a *samanta* or chieftain of Pratāparudra II, who held sway over a district in Krishṇa. It is not possible to say with any certainty whether the epic was composed by Raṅganātha, the court-poet of Buddha Rāzu, in the king's name, or written by the king and dedicated to Raṅganātha. The latter alternative seems to be the more probable; in which case Buddha Rāzu may be regarded as having continued the royal example of Nannechodu and Pratāparudra. The fact that, later in the century, the sons of Buddha Rāzu, Kachavibhudhu and Vittala Rāzu, completed this *Rāmāyaṇa* by adding the *Uttara Rāmāyaṇa*, under instructions of their father, confirms this conjecture. Dvipada, though a somewhat monotonous vehicle for an epic like the *Rāmāyaṇa*, is an easy and graceful medium. The poet's translation is simple, sweet and easily understandable by young and old. It is full of apt similes and pleasing alliterations.

2. **Atharvana** (A.D. 1240– . Title, 'Dvitiyāchārya'). Variously placed towards the beginning and the end of the century by historians, but regarded by tradition as the contemporary of Nanniah, Atharvaṇa is the author of *Triliṅga Śabdānuśāsana*, the Triliṅga grammar. The name Atharvaṇa is regarded by many as not a real name, but an assumed title. The object of the author in writing this grammar is to show the antiquity of Telugu, and he probably thought that the homely name of Nallanna was hardly dignified enough for the purpose. The name does not occur in Āndhra Desa; indeed, Brahmins belonging to Atharvaṇa Śākha are not to be found in the Telugu country, and there are not many in other parts of India. It is probable that the name is assumed to suggest that the language of which he is the grammarian is as ancient as the *Atharva Veda*. The author has the unique distinction of being the only Jain writer in the whole range of available Telugu literature. He is referred to as a standard author by later writers. The poet is also reputed to have written a work on prosody, *Atharvaṇa Chandas*, and he attempted to continue the *Bhārata* from where Nanniah had left it, and actually

finished the *Virāta, Udhyoga* and *Bhīsma Parvas*. For some reason or other, neither of these works has survived, but illustrative stanzas are given from these by Appakavi.

A grammarian is hardly qualified to be a poet; and that may be the reason why Atharvaṇa's *Bhārata* had no chance alongside the brilliant achievement of his contemporary, Tikkanna. Atharvaṇa is called Dvitiyāchārya to distinguish him from Nanniah, who is regarded as the first grammarian, and therefore the first āchārya (Pratham-āchārya). The book is written in Sanskrit, though the subject matter relates to Telugu grammar.

3. **Tikkanna.** The most inspiring personality of this century was Tikkanna, who translated the *Bhārata*, to which reference has been made already. Tikkanna was an octogenarian, and saw the end of the century of which he is the most conspicuous poet.

4. **Mulaghatika Ketana** (A.D. 1250– . Title, 'Abhinava Daṇḍi'). He translated the *Daśakumāracharitra* from the Sanskrit original by Daṇḍi, and dedicated it to Tikkanna. He also wrote a grammar, called *Āndhra Bhāshā-bhūshaṇa*, and translated Vijñāneśvara's commentary on Yājñavalkya's *Smṛiti*, known as *Mitākshara*, the governing authority on Hindu law in South India. As there is no reference to Tikkanna's *Bhārata* by this poet, it may be surmised that he wrote his *Daśakumāracharitra* before Tikkanna began his translation. *Daśakumāracharitra* (the adventures of ten princes) contains stories of common life and reflects a corrupt state of society of that day.

5. **Beddanna** (A.D. 1261–). An Āndhra Choda minor feudatory chief of Shatsahastra land, in the reign of the Kākatīya princess, Rudramadevī. Like his predecessor, Pratāparudra, this king composed a book, *Nītiśāstra Muktāvaḷī*—the pearl chain of political truths—a book dealing with the functions and duties of kings, appointment of officers, administration of justice, functions of the executive and the protection of the country; in all, containing fifteen chapters on the science of politics. Beddanna is said to have been the author of *Sumati Śataka*, a canto of moral maxims, one of the most widely read moral text-books in the Telugu schools. This book, together with *Vemana*

Śataka, supplies in imperishable verse, pointed and pithy, the moral training of the Telugu youth.

6. **Marana,** a disciple of Tikkanna, wrote *Mārkaṇḍeya Purāṇa*, which he dedicated to the minister Nāgayyaganna, Commander of Pratāparudra II. This book ranks very high in the literature of the time. The story of Mārkaṇḍeya is the basis of the *Manucharitra* of Peddana, who has paid Māraṇa the compliment of imitation in many places.

7. **Manchanna,** a contemporary of Tikkanna and a resident of Rajahmundry, wrote *Keyūrabāhucharitra* and dedicated it to Nanduri Gundanna, a grandson of the minister of Pṛithvī Rāja, the last of the Velanādū Chodas.

8. **Hullakki Bhaskara** translated the *Rāmāyaṇa* of Vālmīki into Champu, and dedicated it to Sāhiṇimāra, literally a horseman. This unusual dedication is explained by a story which, as usual, is interesting, though unhistorical. The ruling prince, Buddha Rāzu, asked Raṅganātha to compose the *Rāmāyaṇa*. On hearing this, his minister, Bhāskara, undertook to have a better translation of the same epic done. The king promised that he would accept whichever poem was brought to him first. Bhāskara gave the commission to the poet attached to him, Huḷḷakki Bhāskara. Both Raṅganātha and Bhāskara finished and brought them to the king on the same day. The king, who favoured Raṅganātha, received his composition with his right hand and insulted Bhāskara by receiving his with the left hand. Chagrined at this lack of courtesy, the poet took back his book with the words that he would rather dedicate it to a horseman or a coachman than to a rude king. The king's horseman, hearing this and desiring to have his name perpetuated, requested the author to keep to his word. The story is no doubt a later invention, because, for one thing, Raṅganātha and Mantrī Bhāskara and Huḷḷakki Bhāskara are not contemporaries. Moreover, Sāhiṇimāra is not a coachman, but the son of Buddha Rāzu and a cavalry commander in the imperial army. The story, however, does contain two elements of truth. The dedication to Sāhiṇimāra seems to be an afterthought, and something must have occurred to have changed the poet's mind. The book was obviously written against time. It is a joint product

of Bhāskara and his disciples, written with record speed, probably to overtake a rival in the race.

Fourteenth Century Poets. Five poets, stars of the first magnitude, adorn this century, and it is a pity that the major portion of the heritage they have left is lost and has not come down to us. **Vemalavada Bhima Kavi** is a poet of mystery in Telugu literature. Tradition has been busy weaving stories round his name, so many and so incongruous, that we may well despair of coming to anything like an accurate determination of his date. Variously placed in the twelfth, thirteenth, fourteenth, fifteenth and sixteenth centuries A.D., it may be that he is one of our earliest poets. But the attempt to determine his date by reference to historic persons associated with him by tradition has not been productive of any solid results. The cycle of legends which surround this poet belong to an age when the poet is regarded as an inspired prophet. Such stories in other literatures indicate generally that the poet who has gathered these myths and legends around him, belongs to the twilight of literary beginnings. Moreover, Śrīnātha places him before the Kavitraya; an inexplicable error if he belonged to his own century.

The mystery and uncertainty that hangs round the life of this poet extend to his poems as well. We are not in a position to state with any certainty that he is really the author of any of the books attributed to him. Apart from the fact that he was a staunch Śaivite, nothing is known of him. Five or six books are attributed to him. They are: (1) *Rāghava Pāṇḍavīya*, the story of Rāma and Kṛishṇa, in a double-meaning verse. This book was lost and became a mere memory by the time of Piṅgaḷi Sūranna. (2) *Kavi Janāśraya*, recently printed, is said to be the work of a Jain Komaṭi, Rāchanna. (3) and (4) *Śatakanṭa Rāmāyaṇa* and *Nṛisiṁha Purāṇa* are not extant and are known only by illustrative stanzas given in anthologies. There is an inherent improbability in a Śaivite writing a Vishṇu Purāṇa. (5) It is exceedingly doubtful if the poet wrote the *Vāsava Purāṇa* in Telugu, as there is a Sanskrit work of the same name associated with his name.

Bhīma Kavi flits across the stage like a strange shadow, the centre of myth and miracle, never materialising into a concrete figure of history.

Nachana Soma and Amaresvara. Two other poets, worthy to be ranked with the Kavitraya, have transmitted their reputation to posterity, but without transmitting much of their work which entitled them to fame.

Nachana Soma (A.D. 1355–77). A court poet of Bukka Rāya, an ancestor of Kṛishṇadevarāya, is the author of *Uttara Harivaṁśa*. Probably dissatisfied with Errāpragada's achievement, this poet wrote it in what is considered to be a style worthy of the theme. Competent critics have adjudged that the claim of the poet is made good by the excellence of his composition, which all through maintains the high level of the Kavitraya and, in portions, even surpasses them. The same may be said of Chimmapūdi Amareśvara, whose work, *Vikramasena*, celebrating the victories of King Vikrama of Ujjain, is lost. It is said that we should have had a Kavi Chatushṭa, including this poet with the three translators of the *Bhārata*, had not that name been reminiscent of the memory of the 'wicked four' of the *Bhārata*. The loss of *Vikramasena* is a great literary calamity.

Errāpragada, the third poet who completed the translation of the *Bhārata* ; Vinnakota Peddana, author of a grammar, *Kāvyālankāra Chūḍāmaṇi* ; and Ravipati Tippanna, author of *Tripurāntakodāharaṇa*; *Madana Vijaya* and *Ambikaśatakam* all belong to the same century.

Srinatha (A.D. 1365–1440). The poet who overshadows all others of his age is Śrīnātha, who lived in the latter part of the fourteenth and the first half of the fifteenth century. Impartial criticism assigns to him a position equal to that of the Kavitraya, and there are many who hold that he is the supreme poet of Telugu literature. Unlike Nāchana and Amareśvara, his reputation is not built on unverifiable tradition or fragmentary remnants, but on extensive writings available for criticism. The Telugu language has not produced a poet who had such a phenomenal linguistic command over Telugu and Sanskrit. His *Śṛiṅgāra Naishada* is a crown set with dazzling diamonds on the brow of Sarasvatī. Born of humble parentage in an insignificant village, he carved out a name for himself by the excellence of his genius. His inspiration was unfailing. He never stumbled for a word, nor strained for a sentiment. The peculiar qualities of his style may be said to be majesty and stateliness. The rhythm and cadence of his words have something of the surge of the sea and, like the waves, they roll in serried ranks crested with white. Śrīnātha lisped in verses. While still an infant playing childish games he composed *Marutrat Charitra.* Barely out of his teens, he published *Śālivāhana Sapta Śatī.* In the prime of his youth he gave the world *Naishāda*, his *magnum opus*, and *Bhīmeśvara Purāṇa.* In his mature old age, when the weight of years sat heavily on him, he brought out a kāvya, *Kāśikhāṇḍa*, worthy to be compared in all respects with the productions of his youth. Other Śaivite works of his are *Paṇḍitārādhya Charitra*, which had for its basis Pālakuriki Somanātha's book of that name; *Śivarātri Mahātmya*, recently discovered and published by the *Āndhra Parishad; Vallabhābhyudaya*; *Haravilāsa* and *Śṛiṅgāra Dīpikā*—a work on poetics, which, though purporting to be the composition of Kumāragiri Reddi, is held by many to be by Śrīnātha. In two other poems attributed to him, *Palnāti Vīra Charita* and *Vīdhināṭaka*, he is the pioneer of an untrodden field of literary effort. The first is a saga of the Reddi kings—a romance of love and war among the local tribal lords of his days. Literary history of this type is rare in Telugu.

A far more interesting departure from the beaten track was *Vīdhināṭaka.*[1] Though the existing work of that name is a disgusting combination of high art and low morals, there can be no doubt that the original conception, of which it is the degenerate descendant, had its birth in the fertile imagination of Śrīnātha. *Vīdhināṭaka* in Telugu literature has no resemblance to its namesake in Sanskrit drama, described in the *Daśarūpa. Vīdhināṭaka* contains mostly descriptions of street scenes of Rajahmundry in

[1] The standard work on drama in Sanskrit.

light running verses. The poet gives us an insight into the familiar scenes of city life in his own inimitable way. Then comes a vivid description of the ladies the poet has met in the streets of Rajahmundry in a live-long day.

Of his numerous kāvyas two, which reflect his genius at its best, deserve mention. In the Sanskrit language there are five books, called *Pañchamahā Kāvyas*, which every pandit, with any pretension to culture, is expected to master. They are, the three works of Kālidāsa known as *Kālidāsa Traya*, Bhāravi's *Kirātārjunīya* and Māgha's *Śiśupalavadha.* It is only after the student has studied these five books that he is supposed to be fit to undertake the difficult classic, *Naishada.* There is also a proverb which shows that two books in Sanskrit were regarded as extremely difficult for the student, viz. *Kāsīkhānda Mayahpinda* and *Naishāda Vidvat Aushada.* Few poets were willing to test their skill by undertaking the translation of what are considered by the pandits to be the most difficult kāvyas extant. Śrīnātha essayed this difficult task with remarkable success.

Naishada, which celebrates the fortunes of Nala and Damayantī, was composed in Sanskrit by Śrīharsha. Śrīharsha's book, on account of its difficult style, is called the medicine for the pandit.

'A Śrīnātha for a Śrīharsha'—so goes the proverb. Śrīnātha's translation of this remarkably high-class kāvya excels in places the original itself in beauty. Full of sonorous and sweet *samāsas,* the poem has the complicated symphony of an orchestra. Verses full of sibilant sweetness and labial liquidity abound. Descriptions of women are vivid, delicate and artistic. Lines linger in the memory like forgotten music. The book deserves all the praise which has been bestowed on it.

An interesting story is told in connection with Śrīnātha's *Naishada.* In places, the poet almost transliterates, instead of translates, the original. This gave rise to an amusing incident. Hearing of the astounding knowledge of the boy prodigy, Pillalamarri Pinavīrabhadriah,[1] Śrīnātha

[1] See p. 66.

was anxious to get his opinion of his book. Finding him playing in the street with other boys, Śrīnātha approached him and informed him of his purpose. The boy asked him how he translated the phrase, 'Gami karmi kruta Naikanī Vrutta' in the original. Śrīnātha replied that he translated it as 'Gami karmi kruta Naikanī Vruthuda.' On hearing this the boy critic observed, 'Your only contribution seems to be the syllable "da."' We cannot, of course, take this as serious criticism. However, it illustrates Śrīnātha's fine sense of symphony. Where the original was untranslatable he never attempted it. Moreover, by a slight change just of a letter here and a letter there, Śrīnātha could transform harsh phrases in the original into sweet ones in Telugu. It is a noteworthy fact, illustrative of the essential symphony of Telugu, that Sanskrit when transliterated into Telugu gains considerably in sweetness and music.

Śrīnātha's character seems to have been as full of faults as his style is free from them. Tradition has associated with his name many stories which do not add lustre to his character, and there are aspects of his work which seem to confirm the traditional impression, though much of it may be gross exaggeration. Nevertheless, in Śrīnātha we have a poet worthy to be ranked with the Kavitraya, and one at whose hands Telugu poetry attained a majesty and dignity unapproached ever since.

Fifteenth Century Poets. The closing century of the period of translations witnessed the rendering of the Purāṇas into Telugu, of which the most important is *Śrī-Mad-Bhāgavata*, dealing exclusively with the history of Śrī Kṛishṇa as an incarnation of Vishṇu. It is said that Vyāsa, who composed the Sanskrit *Bhārata*, was not satisfied with the incidental mention of Kṛishṇa therein, and wanted to write an epic exclusively celebrating Kṛishṇa as the hero, and so produced the *Bhāgavata*. The *Bhāgavata* has been regarded as the main sacred book of the Bhakti school and is specially held in high veneration by Vaishṇavites. We may therefore regard the translation of the *Bhāgavata* as the first literary symptom of the influence of Vaishṇavism, which is more perceptible in the second stage of the development of Telugu literature in the reign of Kṛishṇadevarāya.

The word Purāṇa means an ancient story or legend, but in course of time it has come to indicate a literary medium suitable for semi-didactic and semi-devotional themes. As a matter of fact, the subject-matter of a Purāṇa is varied. There are in Sanskrit eighteen chief Purāṇas. All these deal with the cosmogony of the Universe, with incidental references to the history of the world, including India and its future development. Most of these Purāṇas belong to the realistic school of philosophy, which regard creation not as *Māyā* but as the *Līla* of God. We owe the reconstruction of the Āndhra dynastic story to the *Vāyu* and *Vishṇu Purāṇas*. Sometimes a Purāṇa is merely a philosophic exposition of a religion, such as Śaivism or Vaishṇavism, in the form of a dialogue or story narrated by a *ṛishi*. Not infrequently it is the story of a sectarian religion with distinctly mytho-poetic tendencies, like the *Basava Purāṇa*. The proper function of a Purāṇa is said, in the *Mahābhārata*, to be the narration of the genealogy of any great king of antiquity.

We have already seen that in the thirteenth century A.D. Mārana translated the *Mārkaṇḍeya Purāṇa*; and in the fourteenth, Errāpragada translated the *Nṛisiṁha Purāṇa*; Śrīnātha, the *Bhīmeśvara* and *Basava Purāṇas*; and Kamalanābha, grandfather of Śrīnātha, *Padma Purāṇa*. The outstanding poet of the first half of the fifteenth century was Bammera Potana, who translated the *Bhāgavata*.

Bammera Potana (A.D. 1400-75). The author of the *Bhāgavata Purāṇa* was a Niyogī Śaivite. His birthplace has been the cause of a protracted controversy. The honour is claimed by Warangal, capital of Pratāparudra in the Nizam's Dominions, and Ontimitta in Cuddappah. Potana was honoured in his day for his purity, integrity and independence. In this he was a striking contrast to his brother-in-law, Śrīnātha, who lacked the subtle sense of self-respect. Śrīnātha basked in the sunshine of royal favour; Potana avoided kings aud courts. Śrīnātha knew how to turn rhyme into rupees, Potana preferred poverty with honour to riches and wealth;

Śrīnātha dedicated every one of his poems to a king or a rich man; Potana spurned to wed the damsel of poesy to wretched kings for money; Śrīnātha was a courtier, Potana a devotee. Many stories are told of Śrīnātha'a attempts to induce Potana to befriend the mammon of unrighteousness, but he preferred to live and die a poor man, and disdained to bow the knee to kings while he had Śiva to worship and Kṛishṇa to celebrate.

Potana was a self-made and self-taught man. He appears to have had no formal schooling. This is why some defects, counted as such by pandits, are found in his style. It is a signal proof of the devastating influence of criticism on literature that his *Bhāgavata* should not have been regarded by some as a standard work, notwithstanding its bewitching beauty of style and sentiment. It is said that while grazing cattle the poet met a yogī called Jītānanda, by whose blessing he obtained his intellectual awakening and the gift of poetry. In his early days, Potana was a gay young man, a favourite in the court of Rao Singhama, in praise of whose courtesan he composed a rhapsody called *Bhoginī Daṇḍaka*. This was the work of Potana before his conversion. After conversion, he began the translation of *Bhāgavata*. We have already said that the *Bhāgavata* deals with Kṛishṇa. In narrating the incident of Dhaksha Yāga it was necessary to relate the Rakshasās' enmity to Śiva and the words of contumely used by him. As a staunch Śaivite, Potana felt this very much, and by way of atonement is said to have written *Vīrabhadra Vījaya* in praise of Śiva.

Potana's life was devoted to the translation of the *Bhāgavata*, which he dedicated to Rāma. Rao Singhama wished that the book should be dedicated to him, but it is said that Potana, in spite of the persecutions to which he was subjected, would not consent to dedicate his poem to a mere man, though a king. The Telugu *Bhāgavata*, unlike the Telugu *Rāmāyaṇa* and *Bhārata*, is much bigger than the original; and, unlike them also, portions of it are very popular even among the illiterate. *Gajendra Moksha* and *Rukmaṇī Kalyāṇa* are perhaps the most widely read and recited portions in Telugu literature. The style of

Potana is full of Sanskritisms but, for all that, rich in topical interest and local colour. As an inspirational poet he is not excelled by any other, and his *Bhāgavata* is regarded and utilised as a standard manual of devotion.

It would appear that Potana did not publish the *Bhāgavata* in his life-time. He was disgusted with the worldliness of his day and concluded that the public of the time were unworthy to hear his poem. He left it as a heritage to his son, Mallana, with instructions that he should give it—the Pearl of Great Price—to a pure man who had devotion in his heart. Potana's son did not open the box in which the manuscript was deposited, but bequeathed it to his friend, Veligandala Nārayya, who discovered that portions of it were destroyed by Bana worms. The portions so destroyed were completed by Erchūri Siṁganna and Veligandala Nārayya. Later, Haribhaṭ (1660) translated portions of the *Bhāgavata*. We have also the *Bāla-Bhāgavata* by Koneru Kavi. Apart from the *Vishṇu Bhāgavata*, we have another *Bhāgavata* called *Devī Bhāgavata*, which was translated by an early poet, Dammanadora, and later by Śrīrāma Pantulu and Mulugu Pāpayya. Tirupati Venkateśvara Kavulu has also recently published a translation of this work.

Among the contemporaries of Śrīnātha and Potana, the following may be mentioned:

1. Jakkanna (A.D. 1410–). Translated or composed *Vikramārka Charitra*, celebrating the victories of Vikramārka, the King of Ujjain, a patron of Sanskrit literature and a hero much celebrated in history and song.
2. Madiki Siṁganna (A.D. 1420–). Translated the *Padma Purāṇa*, and *Vāsishṭa Rāmāyaṇa*, the tenth canto of *Bhāgavata* and a treatise on politics, called *Sakala Nīti Sammatamu*.
3. Nissenka Kommanna (A.D. 1430–). Wrote *Śivalīlā Vilāsa* and *Vīramaheśvara*.
4. Anantāmātya (A.D. 1434–), author of *Rasābharaṇa*, *Bhoja Rajīyā*, a book of wonder tales, *Ananta Chandas*, a book on prosody.
5. Gouranna Mantri, a minister who composed *Harichandropākyāna*, the story of the prince who never spoke a lie and who, for the sake of truth, lost his throne, wife and liberty; and *Navanātha Charitra*, remarkable as an early instance of the short story. Both of these are in Dvipada.

6. Vinukonda Vallabha (A.D. 1420–). Vinukonda Vallabha was the son of Ravipati Tippanna. This Tippanna was the ruler of a few villages in Muliki Nādū, besides being the keeper of the crown jewels of Harī Hara Rāja. The poet's *Krīdābhirāmamu*, though it purports to be a translation of a drama in Sanskrit by name *Premābhirāmamu*, is really an original composition. The author is the first Telugu poet to translate a drama as a drama, whereas till then Sanskrit dramas were translated as mere kāvyas. *Kṛīdābhirāmamu*, like Śrīnātha's *Vīdhināṭaka*, is a unique piece of literature in Telugu, an original literary mode exceedingly rare. The scene is laid at Warangal. It is the story of the travels narrated by Govinda Māchanna to his friend Komati Vitagrāmaṇi, informing him of the scenes he had witnessed and the adventures he had met while in Warangal. He gives a delightful description of a cock-fight in the streets of Warangal.

Pillalamarri Pinavirabhadriah (A.D. 1450–80). The second half of the fifteenth century produced one poet of outstanding merit, who stands at the close of the era of translations, summing up in himself extraordinary learning in Sanskrit, encyclopædic knowledge of the Vedas and Vedāngas, and a widespread reputation for sanctity. Pillalamarri Pinavīrabhadriah takes his place in the rank of inspired poets who owe their achievements not to laborious training, but to native talents, imparted by the favourite deity. Pinavīra's family tree is adorned with many poets; and if tradition can be trusted, the boy-prodigy had in his tenth year all the massive learning of a pandit of forty. We are told that Śrīnātha, who wanted to have the poet's criticism of his *Naishāda*, had to seek him among boys playing in the street, and could hardly bring himself to believe that the poet whom reputation had made so formidable was a young lad in his teens. Yet, with one shrewd question and a sharp comment, the boy-poet sent Śrīnātha about his business a sadder and wiser man and rejoined his playmates, all unconscious that he had sat in judgment and condemned the greatest poet of the age.[1]

Pillalamarri Pinavīrabhadriah was the court poet of Sāḷuva Narasiṁha Rāzu, who was for some time the commander of Vīrupaksha Rāya, whom he supplanted, and became an independent ruler of Ana-Gonda in Bellary District. The poet was the disciple of Bhāratītīrta Svāmī, through

[1] See p. 61 f.

whose favour he obtained the gift of poetry. Many works are attributed to him, of which the following may be mentioned:

1. *Jaiminī Bhārata.*
2. *Sṛiṅgāra Śākuntala.*
3. *Avatāra Darpuṇa.*
4. *Nāradīya.*
5. *Māgha Mahātya.*
6. *Purushārtha Sudhā Nidhi.*
7. *Mānasollāsa Sāra.*

Of these, only the first two are extant. A story current in connection with the *Jaiminī Bhārata* illustrates the popular idea of the poet's versatility. Vīrabhadriah, like many a great poet, led a wild life in his youth, wasting his substance among women. His brother, a very pious Brahmin, had to admonish him very often, but without effect. Having promised the king to compose *Jaiminī Bhārata*, he neglected the task till the last day, notwithstanding the remonstrances of his brother. On the last day he had a room cleaned and purified, and locked himself in. The members of the family could hear the scratch, scratch of the stylo on the palm-leaves. His brother, curious to know what was happening, peeped through the keyhole and found, to his astonishment, a lady furiously writing at great speed. She stood up and went away when she saw the poet's brother. The story is that Sarasvatī was the consort of the poet and she completed the whole epic in a night. The next day he read his composition in the court, and when the pandits applauded the grace of his diction he openly claimed Sarasvatī as his queen—a claim which the audience regarded as blasphemous. But a woman's voice was heard from behind the curtain which justified the poet's claim. It is possible that among the lady-loves of the poet was a poetess of extraordinary ability, who assisted him in his labours. Whatever value may be attached to this story, it was generally believed in his day that the poet had Sarasvatī at his command.

The court poets correctly characterised his style as the lily that gently unfolds its petals and suffuses the air with its soft aroma.

Among Pillalamarri Pinavīrabhadriah's contemporaries the following may be mentioned:

1. Praudhakavi Mallana (1450–), author of *Rukmangada Charitra* or *Ekādśi Mahātya*—a poem of considerable merit. The poet is said to be the son of Bammera Potana, but this is doubtful.

2. Bhairavakavi wrote *Śrīranga Mahātya*, *Kavi Gajankusa*, a treatise on prosody, and *Ratna Śāstra*. The last is a purely scientific work, in verse, on precious stones.

3. Vennela Kanti Sūranna (1460–), author of the *Vishṇu Purāṇa*, which he dedicated to Raghava Reddi, a Vaishṇavite like himself.

4. Dūbagunta Nārāyaṇa (1470–), translated *Pañchaṭanṭra* in verse. Venkatanātha, who lived a little later, translated the same book. Though this author's *Pañchatantra* is inferior to Venkatanātha's, yet it is an exceedingly readable book. The stories are related in an easy fluent style, at once simple and clear.

5. Namdi Malliah, and Ghanṭa Siṁgiah (1480–). These two poets composed together. Of their work, the more important are *Prabhoda Chandrodaya*, a curious drama of divine knowledge, expounding various systems of philosophy, and *Varāhā Purāṇa*.

6. Duggupalli Duggiah (1480–). This poet is the brother of Śrīnātha's wife. He wrote *Nāchiketopākyāṇa* and *Kāñchīpura Mahātya*.

7. Manu Manchi Bhaṭ. Though his date cannot be fixed with certainty, he probably belongs to the close of this century. He wrote a book on veterinary science—*Haya Lakshaṇasāra*. This book, dealing with the treatment and training of horses, is a translation from Sālihotra's book in Sanskrit. Particular interest attaches to this book, as it deals with a subject supposed to be quite modern.

VII

THE PERIOD OF THE PRABANDHAS
(A.D. 1509 – 1618)

The Reign of Krishnadevaraya (A.D. 1509–30) is a proud chapter in Āndhra history. Politically, under his able leadership, the Āndhras began to revive the glory of Rāja-Rāja-Narendra. The imperial grandeur of Kṛishṇadevarāya's reign was reflected in the republic of letters, by the birth of a literary movement, by far the brightest in history for originality and independence, known as the Kāvya or Prabandha period.

The poet, too, had inspiring themes to perpetuate in song and verse. The Muhammadan wave of conquest, moving downwards, was exercising its irresistible pressure on South India. The invader was at the gates. The defender, whom Providence put forward as the saviour of the country, was none else than Kṛishṇadevarāya. Springing from a petty dynasty on the banks of the Tungabhadra, Kṛishṇadevarāya shot into fame by his remarkable military career. He stemmed the tide of foreign invasion on one side, and on the other consolidated, expanded and established an empire as wide and glorious as any witnessed in the annals of South India. Those were stirring, spacious times, of great heroes and glorious battles, of love and valour, and of splendid victories and spreading dominion—a period altogether cast after the heart of a poet.

The Emperor Krishnadevaraya was a patron of letters, and himself a poet of no mean order. He was also a scholar in three languages—Sanskrit, Kanarese and Telugu. In the intervals of his wars he plunged into literature. The imperial court became the resort of the wandering minstrel and the peripatetic poet. It resounded to a battle of wits and competition of poets as momentous in the history of letters as the glorious military conquests were in the political history of the land. Thus was born, under the most propitious stars, a literary movement which in its youth was the glory, and in its decadence the humiliation, of Telugu literature. This new chapter in our literary history, was inspired and led by Kṛishṇadevarāya.

Up to A.D. 1500, Telugu literature may be characterised as belonging to the age of translations, wherein the poet borrowed his theme both in substance and in detail from the Sanskrit original. The reign of Kṛishṇadevarāya marks the beginning of a new era of literary freedom. Under his insdiring leadership, imitation was exchanged for self-expression. Released from the leading-strings of Sanskrit, the Telugu language celebrated its coming of age by inaugurating the literature of freedom. The kāvya is essentially descriptive, while the epic is fundamentally narrative. The epic depends for its appeal on the events and situations in the story, and the kāvya on the wealth and variety of the descriptive element. The kāvya afforded considerable room for the display of imagination and individual taste. The plot, generally thin, is woven round a significant, but little known, Purāṇic episode. The chief interest lay in the painting of character, the portrayal of passing moods and moving passions, and the analysis of emotion. The epic crowded the canvas with innumerable figures; the kāvya cleared the stage of all but the hero and the heroine, it traced the birth and growth of their love and held a mirror to the changing moods and the elusive hopes and fears of their romance. Another noticeable characteristic is the studied employment of a decorative style, in which certain figures of speech, such as the simile and the hyperbole, play an important part. Allied to this feature is the use of *slesha*, the conjunction of words which give a double meaning. The style is sonorous, with a distinct bias for massing Sanskrit compound words.

Kṛishṇadevarāya most appropriately leads off the movement with his *Amuktamālyada* or *Vishṇuchittīya*. This kāvya is remarkable, not only as the firstfruits of a new movement, but also as a clear indication of the influence of Vaishṇavism on Telugu literature. The works of the first period are predominantly Śaivite; but in *Amukta-mālyada* we have a purely Vaishṇavite story, marking the stage when Vaishṇavism has become the source of poetic inspiration. The plot relates to the life-story of a Vaishṇavite *bhakta*. In the sacred city of Śrī-Villuputtur, in the Pāṇḍya kingdom, there lived a pious Brahmin, Vishṇuchitta, whom the gods chose as the triumphant champion of Vaishṇavism. He found on the banks of a lotus-pond a female child of surpassing beauty, whom he received as a gift from God and reared as his own daughter. This child, Amuktamālyada, was the light of his house and the pride of his heart. When she grew up to womanhood, she began to pine away, for some unknown reason. The secret of her sorrow was her love to Raṅganātha, the deity at Śrīraṅgam. The father, on divining his daughter's affections, took her to the deity, who condescended to receive her as his wife. The celestial household spent the rest of their lives in bliss divine.

The style of Kṛishṇadevarāya is so high and the diction so complicated that the reader is at first repelled rather than attracted. But the persevering student reaps a rich reward. He will find therein customs and religious beliefs of a bygone age vividly portrayed. He will gradually feel the tonic effects of a vigorous style and the glow of a new inspiration. There is hardly a book in Telugu where there is such a continual flow of ideas, seeking an impetuous outlet in language which, though rich, is yet scarcely equal to the task of full and adequate expression. For insight into human nature, and for facility in depicting elusive moods by some striking phrase, Kṛishṇadevarāya has no superior, and scarcely an equal.

Kṛishṇadevarāya was deeply versed in Sanskrit, and he is said to have written the following works in Sanskrit, though none of them are available:

1. *Madālasā Charitra.*
2. *Satya Vadhū Preṇanamu.*
3. *Sakala Kathā Sāra Saṅgraha.*
4. *Jñāna Chintāmaṇi.*
5. *Rāsāmañjarī.*

Rāya's services to Telugu literature are manifold. He composed in Telugu himself, and encouraged other poets to do so, often supplying them with materials and themes for composition; above all, as the hero of many battles, he was the inspiration of his age.

The royal court was adorned with many eminent poets, of whom eight, called the 'Ashṭadiggajās,' or eight elephants supporting the world of literature, have become famous. They are:

1. Allasāni Peddana.
2. Nandī Timmanna.
3. Ayyala Rāju Rāmabhadriah.
4. Dhūrjati.
5. Mādiahgāri Mallana.
6. Piṇgaḷi Sūranna.
7. Rāmarāja Bhūshaṇa.
8. Tenāli Rāmakṛishṇa.

It is almost certain that the last three poets did not write in the reign of Kṛishṇadevarāya, though it is unquestionably true that they, along with the rest, are the classic exponents of the kāvya type of literature.

1. **Allasani Peddana** (Title, 'Āndhra Kavitā Pitā Mahūdu') was the Poet Laureate of Kṛishṇadevarāya's court, and the most illustrious and prominent of the poets of the day. The author of a classic which was regarded as the ideal of kāvya literature, honoured by the king, looked up to for guidance and help by the *literati*, Peddana occupies a unique position in the literary world. His great influence in the royal court, his undisputed eminence as a poet, made him the autocrat of the world of letters. What he laid down was law; what he approved of was fame. While to Kṛishṇadevarāya belongs the honour of being the founder of Prabandha literature, it was Peddana who, with his *Manucharitra*, deflected the course of Telugu literature and made the kāvya the archetypal literary mode for centuries to come.

Peddana's celebrated kāvya, *Svarochisha Manucharitra* (shortly *Manucharitra*), has easily eclipsed all other poetical efforts of the day. The story is an episode from the *Mārkaṇḍeya Purāṇa* relating to Svarochisha Manusambhava. A pious Brahmin of Aruṇāspada, on the banks of the Varuṇa, visits the heights of the Himālayas, traditionally reputed to be the abode of a higher order of beings than men, with the aid of a *mantra* imparted to him by a *sidha*. In his wanderings he attracts the attention of a Gandharva damsel, who falls in love with him, but he does not reciprocate her feelings. A male Gandharva, taking advantage of the situation, assumes the form of the Brahmin, consoles the love-lorn maiden and lives with her. Out of the union was born Svarochisha, who in time becomes a ruler and meets many an adventure, in each of which he rescues a maiden whom he weds. The son of Svarochisha is the second Manu, ruler of Jambudvīpa. The story, as will be seen, is slight, but the main interest lies in the varied descriptions of the natural beauty of the Himālayas, and the delineations of character.

In literary form, *Manucharitra* is of composite structure. The poem reveals in many places the characteristic touch of Śrīnātha, for whom Peddana seems to have entertained great respect. In the description of the hunt, Pillalamarri Pinavīrabhadriah is followed. In the conception of situations, Mārana's inspiration is traceable. In the development of the theme, Kṛishṇadevarāya sets the model. *Manucharitra* well illustrates what we may call 'eclecticism in composition,' a very noticeable feature in latter-day poetry.

Peddana's learning in Sanskrit and Telugu was prodigious and his flow of inspiration sustained. In the weaving of words his skill was extraordinary, as Kākamāni Mūrti justly observed. And yet one or two defects are noticeable. Unities are lacking, and the various parts of the story do not properly articulate. Sweet imagery is meagre, though descriptions are delightful, and conversations cunningly managed.

Peddana followed the royal example of laying under tribute foreign words, especially Kanarese, whenever necessary. This practice, though condemned by purists, is a welcome departure, as it adds to the beauty and symphony of the verse. *Hari Kāthā Śāra*, which is attributed to Peddana, is not extant.

Manucharitra was dedicated to Kṛishṇadevarāya, who

honoured the poet above all others, lavished praise and gifts on him and conferred on him the title of 'Kavi Tāpitā Mahā.' The position which Peddana occupied in the royal court was something akin to that of Nanniah in the Chāḷukyā Court, i.e., that of a personal friend whom the king had made his confidant. Like Nanniah too, he had the privilege of inspiring a new literary movement. Nanniah's fault was his also—jealousy of any rising poet who promised to attract the royal attention.

Many stories are told of the king's regard for Peddana. Kṛishṇadevarāya was so much pleased with *Manucharitra* that he insisted, as a mark of his appreciation, on being one of the pole-bearers of his palanquin. On another occasion the emperor insisted on fixing a golden bangle on the poet's leg with his own hands, as a reward for victory in a literary contest. We find Peddana on his retirement, broken down with age and sorrow, bemoaning his desolation at the loss of his royal friend and patron.

2. **Nandi Timmanna** (popularly known as Mukku Timmana) was the second great poet of the royal court. He was a Niyogī Brahmin of the Aruvela sect and a staunch Śaivite by faith. The life-work of the poet was *Parijātāpaharaṇa*, which he dedicated to King Kṛishṇadevarāya. The story celebrates an incident in the life of Śrī Kṛishṇa, whose efforts to satisfy his rival wives often placed him in embarrassing situations. On one occasion he incurred the displeasure of Satyabhāma, by giving Rukmaṇī the flower from Paradise known as Parijāta. It is said that when Śrī Kṛishṇa fell at Satyabhāma's feet in an effort to appease her, she spurned him with a kick. The tactful husband, pocketing the insult, turned her wrath with the soft answer that he was more sorry that her tender feet should be hurt, than that he should be insulted. To satisfy his angry spouse Śrī Kṛishṇa goes to Svargalōka, and after a desperate battle with the heavenly hosts of Indra, who jealously guard the Parijāta, succeeds in removing the tree to Satyabhāma's palace. The lovers' quarrel was soon composed, and the curtain drops over the happy pair rejoicing in each other. There is a beautiful story told as to the circumstances under which the poet

wrote his kāvya. It would appear that on one occasion Kṛishṇadevarāya had a quarrel with his wife which threatened to develop into a serious breach. The queen was found sleeping wlth her legs towards the head of his portrait on the bed-sheet. This the king construed into a personal insult, and hence the quarrel. The poet, who probably came to the royal court in the retinue of the queen, was asked to intercede. This poem was written to show to the king that great freedom is permitted between lovers and that a wise husband should be slow in fancying insults where none was intended. It is said that the king caught the hint, so delicately conveyed through the poem, and became reconciled to his wife.

The poem is a rare prabandha, full of honeyed words, sweet sentiments and delicate and polished imagery. As a work of art it occupies a very high place in Telugu literature.

3. **Ayyala Raju Ramabhadra Kavi** (also known as Pillala Rāmabhadriah—Rāmabhadriah-Of-Many-Children, on account of his large family). Unable to support his growing family, the poet, it would seem, contemplated suicide, but was dissuaded by his friends. At their advice he went with his family to Vijianagaram, with the desperate resolve to earn a livelihood or die in the attempt. Providence helped him at the outset, for on his entry into the capital, he met with an adventure which brought him a friend, who introduced him to the royal court. Caught in a thunder-storm and drenched to the bone, the poet found in a garden a group of students who were struggling hard at the task set by their master—i.e., to give a description of the physical effects of *virāha* (love-sickness). The poet offered to help them if they could kindle a fire for him. Under the grateful glow of the crackling fire, he composed a stanza which the students presented to their master as their own unaided achievement. Tradition identifies their master with Rāmarāja Bhūshaṇa, author of *Vasucharitra*. The master at once realised that he was dealing with a poet of eminence and asked his students to take him to the stranger. Thus was formed a friendship which secured for the poet an entry into the coveted circle of royal poets.

The poet, at the command of Kṛishṇadevarāya, composed *Sakala Kathā Sāra Sangraha*, a poem in nine cantos containing the famous Purāṇic stories of Rāma Pururāva, etc. The poem was not finished by the time Kṛishṇadevarāya died. After the death of his patron, the poet settled in the court of the nephew of the son-in-law of Kṛishṇadevarāya, and composed *Rāmābhyudaya*.

4. **Dhurjati,** a staunch Śaivite, was also of the select circle. He hailed from Kāḷahastī, and appropriately composed *Kāḷahastī Mahātmya*, a kāvya extolling the virtues of Kāḷahastī as a place of pilgrimage. Kṛishṇadevarāya often wondered at the elegance of his characterisation. Once in the full court the emperor propounded the question, 'Whence did this worshipper of the poison-throated Śiva get this incomparable sweetness of expression?' The answer which the assembled poets gave, while confirming the royal patron's approbation, shows him to be a gay young man with rather doubtful morals. Dhūrjati managed to combine a reputation for profound piety with considerable looseness of character.

5. **Madiahgari Mallana,** another Śaivite poet of the court, was the author of *Rāja Sekhara Charitra*. He was so called to distinghish him from Praudhakavi Mallana.

6. **Sankusala Nrishimhakavi.** Though not counted among the 'great eight', he deserves special mention, as he ranks among the foremost of the poets of the day. The poet wrote *Kavikarṇa Rasāyana*, which he desired to dedicate to the emperor. With this object he approached Peddana, and, after reading to him portions of his work, requested him to introduce him to the emperor. Peddana, jealous of the poet's ability, and apprehensive that his own position might be jeopardised, put obstacles in his way. Disgusted at Peddana's conduct, and unable to obtain an entry into the royal presence, the poet was driven to selling his poem in the open market. One of the stanzas sold reached Mohanāṅgi, the daughter of the emperor. One day, while playing chess, she repeated a stanza from *Kavikarṇa Rasāyana*. The emperor, struck with the beauty and aptness of the stanza, enquired where she got it from and was told that a starving poet sold it in the bazaar. The

emperor was grieved to learn about the plot of Peddana, and wanted to make amends to the poet by permitting him to dedicate his work to him. But this was not to be, as Nṛisiṁhakavi had left the place for Śrīraṅgam, where he dedicated his poem to the goddess of the shrine. Whether the story is true or not, it illustrates the fact that true genius is irrepressible, and in the days of Kṛishṇadevarāya merit never remained unrecognised in the long run. Nṛisiṁha did not suffer fools gladly, and he has devoted a considerable portion of his introduction to the condemnation of incompetent poets.

7 and 8. **Kummari Molla** and **Kumari Dhurjati.** Two other poets of the reign are Kummari Molla, the potter poetess, who composed a *Rāmāyaṇa*; and Kumārī Dhūrjati, who chronicled the conquests of Kṛishṇadevarāya under the name of *Kṛishṇadevarāya Vijaya.* He also composed *Sāvitrī Charitra* and *Indumatī Vivāha.*

Of the minor poets of the time we need mention only the following: (1) Bhāskara Pantulu, who wrote *Kaṇyakāpurāṇa*, the story of the patron saint of a sect of Vaiśyas; and (2) Piduparti Somanātha and Piduparti Basavakavi—two Liṅgāyat poets—authors of *Basava Purāṇa* and *Prabhuliṅga Līla*, respectively.

The latter half of the sixteenth century A.D. was dominated by three poets, Piṅgaḷi Sūranna, Rāmarāja Bhūshaṇa, and Tenāli Rāmakṛishṇa, all of whom, while carrying forward the general movement of kāvya literature, added, by way of individual contribution, new elements and variations. Of these three poets, Piṅgaḷi Sūranna stands out easily the most prominent, by his daring originality, freedom from convention and unique variety of genius. It is natural that the fame of Peddana's *Manucharitra* should have challenged the ambition of that aspiring age. Nrisiṁhakavi, with his *Kavikarṇa Rasāyana*, tried to scale higher altitudes, by including in the range of descriptions a larger variety than Peddana utilised or the rhetoricians demanded. The new claimant for a place in the sun was Piṅgaḷi Sūranna.

Pingali Suranna was a Niyogī Brahmin of Āpastamba Sūtra. His family was originally resident at Piṅgaḷi, a petty village in Kistna District. The poet attached himself to the court of Kṛishṇa Rāzu (a contemporary of Sadaśivarāya, the successor of Kṛishṇadevarāya) of Nandayal. Piṅgaḷi Sūranna's first work which brought him fame was *Rāghava Pāṇḍavīya*—a 'Dvanda Kāvya' in which each verse is capable of giving two meanings, one applicable to the story of Rāma and the other to the story of the *Mahābhārata*—and the whole poem carrying the double story continuously. Piṅgaḷi Sūranna and Rāmarāja Bhūshaṇa may be said to be the pioneers of this kind of literary development, known as 'Slesha' Kāvya. Compared with *Vasucharitra*, *Rāghava Pāṇḍavīya* has one merit, rare in this type of composition, namely, grace and simplicity of style. It is a tribute to the genius of Sūranna that he was able to compose a Dvanda Kāvya which is at once simple and natural—an achievement unapproached by subsequent writers. A peculiarity of this book is that the poet has departed from the time-honoured custom of describing his family history in the introduction. Muddirāju Rāmanna wrote a commentary on *Rāghava Pāṇḍavīya* in the sixteenth century. Next, in order, comes *Kaḷāpūrnodaya*, by common consent a unique production in Telugu literature. We have already noticed that the Purāṇic writers followed a Sanskrit original, and the kāvya writers a Purāṇic episode. A purely imaginary story never was the theme of a great poet. Indeed, the author of *Vasucharitra* condemns kāvyas based upon stories of imagination, as 'inferior diamonds.' Sūranna, in the face of the literary traditions of the day, chose for his *Kaḷāpūrnodaya* a story of his own invention. Rambhā, the most beautiful of celestial damsels, proud of her beauty, boasts that she is peerless and unconquerable and that none can separate her from her lover, Nalakūbera. Nārada, the wanderer in the heavens, foretells her fall, and prophesies that a false Rambhā and Nalakūbera will rise, to confound her pride. Kalabhāshiṇi and Maṇikandhara are destined to play the part of the 'double' to Rambhā and Nalakūbera. The rest is a comedy of errors. Kalabhāshiṇi falls in love with Nalakūbera and Maṇikandhara with Rambhā. Maṇikandhara assumes the form of Nalakūbera, and attracts Rambhā to himself. Kalabhāshiṇi assumes the form of Rambhā and is attracted by Nalakūbera. The false and the real meet in a maze of errors. The spell is broken, everybody realises his folly and makes amends. In the centre of the plot are Kṛishṇa and his seraglio, and in the background are Kāli worshippers with dark hints of human sacrifices, and Malayāḷi magicians with mystic garlands and strange spells. A noticeable feature of this work is that the writer altogether discards slesha.

Prabhāvati Pradyumna is the last of Sūranna's works—the fruit of maturer years. In the previous work we observe that the story is novel, while the treatment follows the traditional path of the kāvya; whereas in *Prabhāvati Pradyumna* the theme is Purāṇic, as in the kāvyas, but the treatment is original. Vajranābha is a *Daitya*, an enemy of *Devas*. He is very powerful, and by virtue of his *tapas* becomes invincible. He resides in a city inaccessible to men and gods. Taking advantage of his invulnerable position, he conquers the three worlds and imperils the position of Indra, who seeks the help of Kṛishṇa to achieve the downfall of the wicked Vajranābha. How to conquer him whom gods have made invulnerable—this is the problem of the gods. See how the divine plotter sets about. Swans are neither gods nor men, and can find entrance into Vajranābha's territory. On this hangs the plot. The Daitya king has a beautiful daughter, Prabhāvati. The wily swan, so useful to the Indian poet, creates in Prabhāvati a love for Pradyumna, son of Kṛishṇa. The daughter of Daityas in love with the son of Devas, —parents sworn to eternal enmity—forms the good old situation. The artful swan sings the praises of a dramatic troupe of Bhadra, far famed in Devaloka. Pradyumna is smuggled with the troupe into the capital of the Daitya king. There follow love scenes, political intrigues; the father is killed, and the daughter is married.

In order to measure the greatness of Piṅgaḷi Sūranna and the literary value of his kāvyas, it is necessary to realise how far he has risen above the limitation of the times. The poet has endeavoured, though not with complete success, to escape the allurements of the kāvya type of literature, then rendered irresistible by the striking successes of a procession of great poets. The besetting sin of the kāvya literature is that it detaches art from life. The characters of the play are so many pegs to hang elaborate descriptions upon. There is neither life, development nor *dénouement*. Sūranna clearly perceived the approaching doom of the kāvya, and has sought to inspire the decaying movement with life. Following the master-dramatists of Sanskrit, Kaḷidāsa and Bāṇa, he infused a strong dramatic interest into the kāvya. As we follow him our attention is attracted to the plot and its beauty, not to the poet and his dexterity, as in the kāvyas. Sūranna creates and evolves; his characters are life-like, their movements spontaneous, their conversations natural and the situations tense and vivid. Unlike the kāvya writers, who invariably follow the chronological sequence of events, Sūranna plunges into the middle of the plot, and makes his characters relate the story. *Prabhāvati Pradyumna* opens with a beautiful description of Dwārka, seen in the haze and glow of the morning sun, from the *vimāna* or flying chariot of Indra high in the sky. Piṅgaḷi Sūranna's chief title to fame is that he made a great effort (consciously or unconsciously) to turn the flood-tide of kāvya into drama—not that he succeeded altogether, but he came very near success. He gave us two kāvyas, unique in Telugu literature, which combine the learning of Peddana and the dramatic interest of Kaḷidāsa and Bāṇa. It is interesting to note that this poet was a contemporary of Shakespeare, and his two plays recall to memory the two dramas of Shakespeare—*Kaḷāpūrnodaya*, the *Comedy of Errors*; and *Prabhāvati Pradyumna*, *Romeo and Juliet*.

Ramaraja Bhushana, as his name indicates, adorned the court of Rāmarāya. The son-in-law of Kṛishṇadevarāya, he seems to have served his apprenticeship under Peddana, and keenly followed the literary career of Piṅgaḷi Sūranna. By the time the poet started his literary life, *Manucharitra* was the praise of the *literati* of the day, and *Rāghava Pāṇḍavīya* was the talk of critics. This inspired him with an ambition to take the public by storm with a work which would eclipse the fame of Peddana and Sūranna. He concentrated in his work on the reproduction of the descriptive excellence of Peddana, and the slesha novelty introduced by Sūranna. In this the poet succeeded beyond all expectations and his *Vasucharitra* became the model for the poets who followed him. The rehabilitation of Piṅgaḷi Sūranna is the achievement of modern literary criticism. Tradition makes Rāmarāja Bhūshaṇa the hero of the kāvya stage, and in the opinion of many conservative critics, the pupil is regarded as having excelled his master.

For a prabandha, the theme must be a well-known Purāṇic story. It will be realised that in such a case the freedom of the poet is considerably restricted, as he has to adapt himself to the framework given to him, and his imagination can be exercised only within the limitations of the general outline of the story. This is obvious in the construction of *Manucharitra*. Rāmarāja Bhūshaṇa strained at the leash. He wanted greater freedom than the selection of a Purāṇic story would permit. The new-born urge for freedom demanded not only liberty of expression and latitude in treatment, but complete freedom to shape the subject-matter of the story as well. On the other hand, he was not prepared to go to the extent of Piṅgaḷi Sūranna in discarding the Purāṇic story altogether. His own conception of the kāvya is stated thus: 'Purely imaginary stories are an inferior type of precious stones; but borrowed themes make artificial diamonds. I should like to take a story neither famous nor purely imaginary; but one which is insignificant in itself, while permitting considerable scope for improvement, like a rough precious stone which shines when cut and polished.'

In pursuance of his own canon, the poet chose an insignificant episode from the *Bhāgavata Purāṇa* as the basis of his kāvya. The incident chosen is the marriage of Garika, the daughter of Sūktimatī (a river), and Kolāhāla (a mountain), with the King Vasu—rather a meagre plot. But Rāmarāja Bhūshaṇa handled the theme with infinite skill, making an ingenious use of slesha.

The supreme felicity with which he handles slesha, avoiding wooden artificiality on one side and sacrifice of sense for sound on the other, makes him a supreme artist of this school. But while he owns the same command of expression and felicity of phrase, his style lacks the simplicity of his illustrious colleague, Piṅgaḷi Sūranna.

The primary defect of *Vasucharitra*—a defect inherent in the kāvya type of literature, but more apparent in *Vasucharitra* than in *Manucharitra*—is the over-elaboration of the descriptive element, which smothers the movement of the story, in itself very thin. Descriptions, delightful in themselves, stand out of relation to the immediate demands of the narrative. As one critic justly observes, 'Peddana strings his pearls into a necklace and throws it round the neck of Saraśvatī, while Rāmarāja showers them loose and unstrung on her.'

Rāmarāja Bhūshaṇa had one advantage over his contemporaries. He was himself a great and accomplished musician. This accounts for the symphony and cadence of his verse. There is not only a unique wedding of sound to sense, but also a sweet atmosphere of harmony about his poem. His poetry is song set to music. *Vasucharitra* is a gem of art. Rāmarāja Bhūshaṇa composed also another kāvya known as *Harischandra Nalopākhyāna.* In it he tells simultaneously the adventures of Nala and the suffering of Harischandra, in verse capable of yielding both stories.

There is another book, *Narasabhūpālīya*, about whose authorship critical opinion is divided. Some are of opinion that this is the work of Rāmarāja Bhūshaṇa, while others attribute it to a poet called Bhaṭṭumūrti. Two facts are clear: (1) that Bhaṭṭumūrti wrote *Narasabhūpālīya*, and (2) that Rāmarāja Bhūshaṇa wrote *Harischandra Nalopākhyāna* and *Vasucharitra.* The question that has given rise to the controversy is, whether they are different poets, or different names of the same poet. Rāmarāja Bhūshaṇa is an honorific title, meaning the ornament of Rāmarāja's court; while Bhaṭṭumūrti is a natural name. Contemporary writers have regarded them as the name and title of the same person. Internal evidence tends to the same conclusion. But the genealogies given in the books slightly differ. This is not fatal to the theory of identity.

The suggestion that the author was given in adoption to another family accounts for the difference in genealogy. Sound critical opinion inclines in favour of Bhaṭṭumūrti and

Rāmarāja Bhūshaṇa being the same person. *Narasabhūpalīya* is a treatise on rhetoric in verse. It is a Telugu rendering of *Pratapārudrīya.*

Tenali Ramakrishna. An enigmatic figure of the time was Rāmakṛishṇa, who was attached to the court of Venkatapati Rāya, one of the Vijayanagar kings, who changed the capital of the empire to Chandragiri. Rāmaliṅga, as he was originally called, is said to have been a Śaivite by birth and wrote in his youth the *Liṅga Purāṇa.* However, he became a convert to Vaishṇavism, and changed his name to Rāmakṛishṇa. He is known to posterity, not so much as a poet, but as a court jester, whose practical jokes, witty sallies and resourceful pranks have been ever since the chief source of mirth in family circles all through the Āndhra country. He is generally regarded as a mediæval court jester, with a dash of the 'Charlie Chaplin' in him. He was the contemporary of Tātachāri and Appiah Dīkshit, protagonists of Vaishṇavism and Śaivism respectively. Rāmakṛishṇa was never so happy as when he made the life of the orthodox Tātachāri miserable with his practical jokes. The saving grace of humour often stood him in good stead, as it saved him from the wrath of his royal master, who was himself not infrequently the victim of his irrepressible humour.

As a poet he reveals altogether a new personality; serious, pious and devotional. His great work, *Pāṇḍuraṅga Mahātmya,* contains a legendary account of a shrine of Vishṇu as Pāṇḍuraṅga, at Pāṇḍharpur, consecrated by the ministration of Saint Pāṇḍarika. A Brahmin, Nigama Sarma, who wasted his life in dissipation and debauchery, breathed his last at Pāṇḍharpur. A controversy ensues between the servants of Yama and the servants of Vishṇu; the former were anxious to carry him to hell, as he lived a wicked life, and the latter claimed him for heaven, as he died in that sacred place. Of course, the verdict was in favour of the servants of Vishṇu. Rāmakṛishṇa's work is a kāvya of high merit, remarkable for its sonorous dignity of phrasing, and is justly counted as one of the *Pañcha Mahā Kāvyas* (the Five Great Kāvyas).

OTHER WRITERS

Minor poets belonging to the second half of the sixteenth century A.D., who deserve mention, are:

(1) and (2) Addaṁki Gangādhara, who wrote *Tapatīsamvaraṇa*; and Ponnikanti Telaganārya, author of *Yāyāti Charitra*, a pure Telugu work. Special interest attaches to these books, as they are the only kāvyas in Telugu literature dedicated to a Muhammadan ruler, Ibrahim Mulk, the fourth son of Kutumb Shah, one of the Bahmanī kings, who ruled over Golkonda between A.D. 1512 and 1543. On the death of his father, Ibrahim Mulk incurred the displeasure of his elder brother, and sought refuge under Kṛishṇadevarāya. He was very fond of Telugu literature and was a patron of the poets Gangādhara and Telaganārya, who were attached to his court.

(3) Sāruṅgu Timmanna, the Madhva poet, who wrote *Vaijayanti Vilāsa* or *Vipranārāyaṇa Charitra*, which is a story of a Vaishṇava *bhakta*, whom two sisters of the prostitute class, Madhuravāṇī and Devadevī, tried to seduce from his chastity and almost succeeded, when Vishṇu stretched forth his hand to save him. Chadalavāda Malliah, a descendant of Errāpragada, one of the Kavitraya, also put this story into verse in 1585.

(4) Turagā Rāmakavi earned the unenviable notoriety of being the master of vituperative verse, and was counted as one of the 'cursing poets,' whose maledictions were more effective than benedictions. He dedicated his work, *Nagara Khānda*, to a rich goldsmith named Mārkaṁdeya.

(5) Tarigopulla Mallana, author of *Chandrabhānu Charitra* (1586–1614), was attached to the court of Venkatapati Rāya. The story is about the marriage of Chandrabhan, the son of Kṛishṇa, with Kumudinī, the daughter of Rukmabahu. The poet was a Madhva.

(6) Kamsāli Rudrakavi (A.D. 1620–), a goldsmith by caste, author of a high-class kāvya, *Nirankusopākhyāna*.

The period under survey presents kāvya literature at its best. In the hands of the Ashṭadiggajās, the classic exponents of this type, it became an indigenous movement of great originality. The kāvya literature could have given us (if its early promises had been redeemed) what Telugu literature very much lacks—a nature-school and a psychological school of poetry. It has, in fact, given to our poets a splendid opportunity for self-expression and for the display of individual ability. The kāvya stands for a vivid portrayal of men and nature, a profound study of character and emotion, and for artistic decoration and choice ornamentation. In technique, it marks an endeavour to extract from the Telugu language a new music. Symphony was its soul.

The defects of the kāvya literature are stamped on its face. It is artificial and ornate, with a complicated technique. If it is to be effective, it involves a delicate balance of its component parts, a just sense of proportion, and, above all, a capacity for restraint, which is rarely to be found in any but great masters. It is a complicated machine, so nicely balanced that none but experts can handle it. Piṅgaḷi Sūranna was correct when he diagnosed the condition of kāvya as 'suffering from creeping paralysis,' and pronounced that it could only be saved by an infusion of new life, in the shape of dramatic interest. Unfortunately, Sūranna had no followers.

VIII

THE PERIOD OF STAGNATION
A.D. 1630–1850

THE battle of Taḷikoṭa (1565) is as much a literary as an historical landmark in the life of the Āndhras. It marked the disintegration of the empire founded by Kṛishṇadevarāya, and 'the beginning of the end' of the literary movements inaugurated by him. The Kāvya movement outlived his political downfall for nearly half a century; as the poets, born and trained during the spacious days of the emperor-poet, continued to inspire the movement and maintain it on the same high level. But from the third decade of the seventeenth century, up to the beginning of the twentieth, it is one long night. During this period we find versifiers innumerable, but poets few; literary output enormous, but quality very poor. There is a thick growth of rank vegetation, but hardly a noble tree showing itself. It is an age of stagnation and deterioration. The single redeeming feature of the situation is the extension of the field of Telugu literature to the South. The new literary output came from Tanjore, Madura, Pudukkota and Mysore, and it was marked by distinguishing features of its own. As it stands in clear contrast to the main current, the Northern school, it has been designated as the Southern school.

The primary causes for the steady decline of the Northern school were:

1. **The Disintegration of the Empire of Vijayanagar** into petty pāḷayams under chieftains incompetent to direct any literary movement, since they themselves possessed very little culture or education. Petty patrons beget petty poetry. The poets consequently lack inspiration, vision, vital energy and true ambition.

2. **The Dictatorship of the Grammarian and Rhetorician.** The great poets of the Purāṇa Yuga were the creators of grammar and rhetoric. The poets of the kāvya age were superior to these secondary arts. It is otherwise with the writers of the seventeenth and eighteenth centuries. The kāvya poetry involved a poetic architecture so technical and complicated that the poet had to be apprenticed to the rhetorician in order to learn the new craft. The free spirit of poetry was harnessed by the rhetorician, and the literature suffered under the cramping influence of the 'regulative science.' This accounts for the lack of freedom and spontaneity and for the dull mediocrity of all poetic effort.

3. **The Inherent Vices of the Kavya Style.** The kāvya is the worst literary mode for imitation; and imitation was in the blood of the Telugu poets. The virtues of kāvya are hidden, and its weaknesses glitter on the surface. The imitator caught the latter and missed the former. In its technique, apparently (though not in reality) art was divorced from life. Kāvya emphasised description, and description in turn depended on simile and hyperbole (*upamāna utprekshā*). Simile requires an insight into nature and a gift of imagination, if it is to be original and striking; while hyperbole, to be pleasing, has to be handled with discretion and restraint. The great masters, while they seemed to be engrossed with the technique, really kept an eye on life. Their imitators did not catch this art. They lost touch with nature. They borrowed not only art but also life from the Ashṭadiggajās.[1] The result was that the range of ideas and the nature of ornamentation became stereotyped. The only avenue possible for individual distinction lay in extravagance and aberration. The similes became far-fetched, pointless and abstruse. Hyperbole degenerated into unmeasured exaggeration. One poet said that the turrets of the city seemed to kiss the sky. Another went a step further and imagined that they pierced the vault. Yet a third outstripped these, describing them as emerging in the court of Indra!

[1] See above, p. 72.

Ornamentation was another source of degradation. Nothing is so easy, yet nothing is such bad taste, as overdoing or parading ornamentation. Slesha, alliteration, chitra, kavitva,[1] if occasionally resorted to, add to the beauty and excite interest; but as the sole basis for a kāvya, they are in execrable taste.

The literature of this period, in consequence, moves in one dead level of mediocrity, and monotony is the dominant note. The endless procession of kāvyas, one resembling the other, tire the eye. The old Purāṇic stories are told and retold with prolixity and verbosity. Thought becomes stagnant and the same similes and ideas appear again and again in new garbs. But for the incomparable grace and melody of the language, the poet resembles the 'club bore,' who inflicts on his unhappy victim his favourite story for the hundredth time. The only features which attract our attention are the aberrations, which, strangely enough, meet with the approval of the critics.

The deviations from the norm may be classified under the following heads:

1. **Slesha Kavyas.** The author of *Vasucharitra*, by producing a Dvanda kāvya[2]—a novel type of literary effort—created false tastes and diverted poetic energy into new but unprofitable channels. *Vasucharitra* became the measure of learning and the test of poetic excellence. This gave rise to a crop of imitations, some possessing the merits of *Vasucharitra*, others managing to reproduce all its defects but none of its excellence. Abbanā Mātyā's *Kavi Rāja Manorañjana* (1780), Sūrakavi's *Kavi Jana Rañjana* (1780), Kṛishṇa Kavi's *Śakuntalā Pariṇaya* (1799), and Chāmakūra Venkata Kavi's *Vijaya Vilāsa*, though not slesha kāvyas, fall under the former category. Kūchimanchi Timmanna's *Rasika Janobhirāma*, Podūri Peda Rāmā Mātyā's *Śivarāmābhyudaya*, Sūryaprakāsa Kavi's *Kṛishṇārjuna Charitra* (1850) fall under the latter. The last two are Dvanda kāvyas.

Yet others, in an effort to excel, produced poems capable of telling *three* stories simultaneously. These poems attempt to tell the stories of Rāma and Kṛishṇa and the Pāṇḍavas, and combine the *Rāmāyaṇa*, the *Māhabhārata* and the *Bhāgavata*. Of these the following deserve mention.:

(1) Elakūchi Bālasaraśvatī, *Rāghava Yādava Pāṇḍavīya*.
(2) Nellūri Rāghavakavi, *Yādava Rāghava Pāṇḍavīya*.
(3) Ayyagāri Vīrabhadrakavi, *Rāghava Yādava Pāṇḍavīya*.
(4) Origanti Somasekhara Kavi, *Rāmakṛishṇārjuna Nārāyaṇīya*.

[1] See p. 89. [2] See p. 78.

This type of literature is not easy to write ; it demands infinite resource, phenomenal command of language, and extraordinary ingenuity. But the very restrictions under which the author had to work forbade any poetic quality of a high order. Though looked upon at the time as high-class literature, it does not appeal to modern tastes.

2. **Pure Telugu Poetry.** There is in the modern Telugu language only a residuum of original Telugu. This Dravidian basis is so little that it is not adequate for the composition of even a few verses. If only Sanskrit equivalents are excluded and the rest regarded as pure Telugu, it may be possible, with some difficulty, to compose an all-Telugu kāvya. Poets of the first period, as a curiosity, used to introduce an occasional stanza or two containing pure Telugu words—a feat much appreciated by the readers.

Ponnikanti Telaganārya (1578) made an attempt at opening a new field, by composing his *Yāyāti Charitra*, a kāvya of five cantos, in pure Telugu, avoiding Sanskritisms as far as possible. Curiously enough, he was able to produce a very readable book of considerable merit. Others followed, but not with the same amount of success. Adidamu Bala Bhāskara's *Rāmāyaṇa* (not now available), Kūchimanchi Timmanna's *Rāmāyaṇa* and *Nīlasundarā Pariṇaya* belong to this order.

These works are more or less of the nature of a *tour de force*. The language, involving tiresome circumlocution, is unintelligible even to the pandit. They are like letters written in cypher, unmeaning without a key. In Tamil and in English, the desire to exclude foreign words came in the wake of a purist tendency and was partly the outcome of genuine patriotism. It was not so in Telugu. These writings owe their origin to a frantic effort, on the part of the poet, to hold the flickering attention of his audience by doing something out of the way. These laborious products of misplaced zeal, never read (in fact, not even readable), may be consigned to the literary museum as momentoes of an antiquarian age.

3. **Chitra and Bhanda Kavitva.** Slesha kāvyas and 'Acchā Telugu' works may be considered as literature, though not of a high order. The same cannot be said of developments in other directions, euphemistically called 'fancy poetry,' but really a type of freak literature.

Some poets have composed kāvyas excluding labials. Kottalanka Mrutyumjaya Kavi's *Nala Charitra* and Mariṁganti Siṁgarāchārlu's *Daśaratha Rāja Nandana Charitra* are instances. Others attempted fantastic combinations and produced pure Telugu, non-labial and 'all-verse' kāvyas. Poets are not wanting who carried their self-denial further still and eschewed gutturals along with labials. Extremists of this school discarded the first twenty letters of the alphabet and used only the *apañchavargīya*, i.e., the last five letters. Kāṇāda Peddana Somayājī perpetuated this monstrosity in his *Sesha Śailesā Līla*. The climax of this form of lunacy was reached when stanzas were written in a single letter. Gaṇapavarapu Venkatakavi and Gudāru Venkatadāsakavi are said to have scaled the heights of perfection in this art.

Another variety of chitra kavitva is known as *Garbha* and *Bhanda Kavitvā*. The former involves introduction of stanzas of one metre within another of a different type; the latter consists in fitting short poems into geometrical figures—such as serpents and chariots.

It is difficult to appreciate the tastes of an age that applauded these tongue-twisters and tumblers as poets of merit.

PROMINENT POETS

Seventeenth Century Poets. We have already mentioned some of these in connection with slesha and chitra kavitva. Very few poets of merit are found between A.D. 1630 and 1700. Elakūchi Bālasaraśvatī, a learned scholar who obtained the title of Mahāmahopadhāya, composed a drama called *Raṅga-Kaumudi*. Hari Bhaṭ, about the middle of the seventeenth century, wrote *Varāha* and *Matsya* Purāṇas; Kākamāni Mūrti, often confounded with Bhaṭṭumūrti, is regarded as combining in his style the excellences of Peddana, Timmana and Rāmakrishṇa. He was the author of *Pāñchāli Pariṇaya*, *Rāja Vāhanavijaya* and *Bahuḷāsva Charitra*. Nūtanakavi Sūranna, towards the close of the century, wrote *Dhanābhi Rāmamu* and a drama, *Vishṇu Māya Vilāsa*. *Dhanābhi Rāmamu* embodies the beautiful story of a contest between Manmadha, god of beauty, and Kubhera, god of wealth, as to which of these commands the hearts of men.

Eighteenth Century Poets. Paidimarri Venkatapati opens the century with *Chandraṅgada Charitra*. Kūchimanchi Timmanna, known as Abhinava Vāgānuśasana, wrote many kāvyas, of which *Rukmaṇī Pariṇaya*, *Rājasekhara Vilāsa*, *Baḷḷaṇa Charitra* may be mentioned.

Vakkalanda Vīrabhadranna, who adapted two stories from Sanskrit writers, *Vāsavadatta Pariṇaya* and *Gourī Kalyaṇa* is mentioned with evident appreciation and respect by contemporary writers. One satirist, Kūchimanchi Jaggakavi, and two Christian poets,[1] Mangaḷagiri Ānandakavi, author of *Vedānta Rasāyana*, and Piṅgaḷi Eḷḷanaryundu, who wrote *Tobhya Charitra*, flourished about the same time. The first half of the century closes with Ēnugu Lakshmaṇakavi, who wrote *Rāma Vilasa* and translated into Telugu *Subhāshita Ratnāvaḷi*.

In the second half of the century, Adidamu Sūrakavi (1780), author of *Kavi Jana Rañjana*, popularly known as *Pilla Vasucharitra*; Kanuparti Abbanāmātya, author of *Anuruddha Charitra* and *Kavi Raja Manorañjana*, generally regarded as the best book after *Vasucharitra*; and Dittakavi Nārāyaṇa, who celebrated in verse the Bobbili war between the Rāja of Vijayanagar and the French in Northern Circars in 1756, are conspicuous.

Nineteenth Century Poets. Besides those already referred to, the following may be mentioned:

1. Pindiproli Lakshmaṇakavi, author of *Rāvaṇa Dommīyamu*, or *Laṅkā Vijaya*, (1840–).

[1] See below, pp. 105 ff.

2. Shistu Kṛishṇamūrti, a scholar of considerable learning in Sanskrit, also a musician of considerable ability. He was good at extempore composition and was exceedingly popular as a reader of Purāṇas. He wrote *Sarva Kāmadā Pariṇaya* and many other works.

3. Māda Bhāshi Venkatācharlu was an intellectual prodigy. It is said that he could repeat anything that was read to him twice, upside down. He composed *Bhāratābhyudaya*.

4. Gopinātha Venkatakavi (1850) was the author of a translation of *Vālmīki Rāmāyaṇa*, *Śiśupala Vadha* and *Bhāghavatgītā*.

5. Sonṭi Bhadradri Rāmaśāstri (1860) composed *Chitra Sīma*, an original production in verse on the lines of Piṅgaḷi Sūranna's *Kaḷāpūrnodaya*, a commentary to *Ahobalīyā* and *Śrirāma Śataka*.

THE SOUTHERN SCHOOL

Kṛishṇadevarāya appointed deputies for each of the southern countries he had conquered. On the fall of the empire of Vijayanagar, they became independent rulers of the countries under their control. The task of consolidation took a good part of the century. Their political position secured, they were able to turn their attention to the peaceful arts of literature. It is fortunate that the viceroys appointed by Kṛishṇadevarāya were, like himself, imbued with a taste for literature, and their descendants turned out to be great patrons of art, zealous of their mother-tongue and anxious to conserve Āndhra culture for the colonists. The Southern school was born in a praiseworthy effort to transplant the home culture into the country of their adoption. The literature of the South belongs, partly, to the seventeenth and mostly to the eighteenth centuries A.D. The contributions came from Tanjore, Madura, Puddukota and Mysore.

1. **Tanjore.** Chavva Rāju was the chief appointed for Tanjore by Kṛishṇadevarāya. His son, Achyuta Nāyak, had for his minister Govinda Dīkshit, a Telugu pandit of great learning. It was in the court of Raghunātha (1630–40), son of Achyuta, that the first-fruits of the new harvest were gathered. The king himself composed a prose kāvya, *Valmīki Charitra*. Chāmakūra Venkatakavi, who was attached to the court, gave to the world *Sārangadhara* and *Vijaya Vilāsa*. The former of these two is admired for the vivid, tragic interest of the theme and the impressive

realism of the art; the latter is, perhaps, the last work of real merit in Telugu literature. It has been described as a heap of precious gems. The polish of the language, the delicacy of sentiment, and the melody of verse combine in this poet as in no other. His style is so uniquely his own that a new name had to be coined to express its quality and it was called after his surname, 'Chāmakūrapāka'—Chāmakūra being also the succulent Indian curry. It is probable, though not certain, that Kavi Choudappah—a moralist who stands next to Vemana and Sumati, among Śataka writers—belonged to this period.

Later, Muddupaḷaṇi, a courtesan of Pratāpa Sinha, of Tanjore (1765), composed in Telugu a kāvya under the name *Rādhikā Svantam*. Kasturi Raṅga Kavi dedicated his *Raṅgara Chandamu* to Ananda Raṅgapillai. But the greatest gift of Tanjore to the Āndhra literature is Tyāgarāja, the hymnologist and musician whose songs are sung all over South India.

2. **Madura.** But it is in the eighteenth century and in the court of Vijaya Raṅga Chokkanātha, the king of Madura, a descendant of Nigama Nāyak, appointed by Kṛishṇadevarāya, that we find the Southern school in full bloom. Viśvanātha Nāyak, father of Chokkanātha, is said to have brought many learned pandits from the north, and gave them gifts of land, thus inducing them to settle in the south. The fruits of Viśvanātha's foresight were reaped by his son, Chokkanātha, who set a good example by rendering into prose *Śrīraṅga Mahātya*. Of the group of poets whose literary output not only constitutes the bulk of Southern Telugu literature but also gives the tone to the movement, Samukha Venkata Kṛishṇappa Nāyak has to his credit not less than four books, of which *Jaimini Bhārata*, in prose, may be taken as an example of the high level of literary value attained by the Southern school. *Ahalyā Samkraṇdana*, *Sārangadhara Charitra* and *Rādhikā Svantam* are his other kāvyas. They belong, every one of them, to the erotic type. Sesham Venkatapati's *Tarāśasanka* belongs to the same order. The other works of the period are of a religious type. Syāmakavi is the author of *Rāmāyaṇa* in Vachana, Tupākula Ananta Rāju composed *Vishṇu*

Purāṇa and *Bhāgavatgītā*. Sumati Rāmabhadra Kavi wrote *Hālāsyā Mahātya* and Velagapūdi Kṛishṇa Kavi, *Vedānta Sāra*.

3. **Puddukota.** Puddukota's contribution under Rāja Rāghava Tondamān (1767–89) takes the shape of dictionaries and anthologies among other things, of which Nudurupati Venkatanāryudu's *Āndhra Bhāshārṇava* deserves mention. His son is responsible *for Bilhaṇīya*.

4. **Mysore.** Vīrarāju (1650–1700), whose *Bhārata* is perhaps the earliest extant instance of a prose kāvya, and Nanja Rāju, a minister of the Mysore king, author of *Liṅga Purāṇa* and *Hālāsya Mahātya*, represent the contribution from Mysore.

A bare description of the literature of the period throws into prominence some characteristic features of this school.

1. The chief merit of the Southern school is *the discovery of prose*. During the Purāṇic period we find Nanniah, the first of the Kavitraya, using prose which is simple and clear; but Tikkanna seemed to have scorned any resort to prose in his *Nirvachanottara Rāmāyaṇa*, an example which had some following. Prose is used as a literary device by the classic writers, partly as a 'pause,' to relieve the strain of composition, and partly to traverse portions of the story more rapidly with a view to economy. Writers who follow the Kavitraya, especially Nāchana Soma, and Potana, the author of a *Bhāgavata*, employ a prose style which is afflicted with all the infirmities of poetic composition—complexity, over-ornamentation, slesha and yamaka.

The unique distinction of the Southern school is that it has realised that prose is as valuable and as useful a medium of literary expression as verse. The extensive use of prose was to a large extent dictated by the necessities of the case. The third and fourth generation of Telugus in a Tamil country are not likely to have possessed sufficient education to understand the prabandha or even epic poetry. If, then, culture was to be retained at all, it had to be conveyed through a medium not altogether beyond the comprehension of the average educated man. Prose was obviously such a medium. Nevertheless, the high artistic value and the relatively important place assigned to prose by the writers themselves, show that they understood its function and possibilities. *Jaimini Bhārata* is a work of art, regarded by its author himself as of equal importance with *Sārangadhara*.

2. Secondly, *the deliberate and decidedly more extensive use of the drama* is another feature of the Southern school. During the first three centuries the Northern school did not produce more than two dramas of any importance, and even these do not occupy a noticeable position in the literature of the times. But, according to a recent writer, the dramas of the Southern school, during the eighteenth century alone, exceed twenty in number. Doubtless none of them were of any acknowledged literary value. But that is also the case with the Northern school. Here again the use of the drama may have been adopted in order to bring the Āndhra culture to those who had not even the capacity to understand prose. In any case, in one century, the Southern school produced more dramas than the Northern school in the course of eight centuries of its existence.

3. The most arresting feature of the Southern school is *the absence of ethical principles.* To whatever causes we may attribute it, the fact is undeniable that the Southern school is essentially immoral. This is brought out by the examination of a characteristic feature of the literature of this period. Excluding directly religious topics, there is hardly a poet, whether of the Northern or Southern school, who did not write a kāvya dealing with the marriage of the heroes of the Purāṇas. We may say that ninety per cent. of the books deal with Pariṇaya, Kalyāṇa or Vivāha. This preoccupation with the question of marriage is the central fact of interest. The mystery of sexual attraction has always been the theme of the poet and the painter. But the way in which they deal with it is indicative of the culture of the age. The poets of the Purāṇa Yuga deal with it with delicacy, reverence, and a sense of its spiritual significance. The hero wins his bride either in a contest of valour or on the battlefield. He seals his faith in the nobility of womanhood by risking his life. The writers of the kāvya period fall far below the ideal. By stressing 'Śṛingāra Rāsa,' they have impaired the subtle aroma of

social relations. Physical attractions are described with an elaborate minuteness and a wealth of detail repulsive to delicate feeling. Even the loves of gods, forbidden to the poets by the writers on poetics, are not immune from their prying attentions.

The Northern school, even in its wildest excesses, never departs from the conventions of life. The sexual attraction finds its legitimate consummation in marriage, though marriage is regarded as the end rather than the beginning of all romance.

But the Southern school stands in painful and humiliating contrast to the Northern in this matter. The poets do not so much deal with marriage as with the violation of chastity. Their treatment of the problem recalls to the mind the unconventional modern schools of Shaw and Ibsen ; only they lack the earnestness of purpose or coherent philosophy of the modern schools ; and they are prurient, often putrid. These poets preach immorality as a creed, in kāvya and drama, in prose and poetry, in song and story. The prominent works of this period are *Sārangadhara*, *Tārāśaśaṅka*, *Bilhaṇīya* and *Rādhikā Svānta*. The story in the first comes very near the tragedy of incest. Rāja-Rāja-Narendra takes for his wife, in his old age, one who cherishes in her heart a love for his son. Her advances are rejected by Sārangadhara. She, in turn, trumps up a false charge against him and throws him to the wolves. *Tārāśaśaṅka* is the story of Chandra's elopement with his guru's wife. *Bilhaṇīya*, a story which counts more than five authors, relates to the same theme in another aspect. King Madanabhirāma appoints Bilhaṇa to teach his daughter, Yaminī Pūrṇa Tilaka. The teacher is beautiful and the daughter young, and to prevent complication he tells his daughter that the teacher is born blind and informs the teacher that his pupil is a leper. A curtain separates the teacher from the pupil. But, one day Bilhaṇa describes the rising moon and gives away the show. The result is not marriage but free love. It is the same with the literary stories of the period. *Śuka Saptati* and *Haṁsaviṁśati* relate the artful way in which society women violated their marital vows.

It is easy to dismiss the whole outlook as immoral putrifaction. But when we set the Southern against the Northern school, it is difficult to escape the conviction that some social upheaval has thrown into relief the problem of sexual relations, which the Northern school deals in a conventional, and the Southern in an unconventional, way. As we read we are led to ask 'Is it pruriency or philosophy?' or, 'Is the problem of the "eternal triangle" not quite so modern as we sometimes suppose?'

IX

POPULAR LITERATURE

THE impulse for the translation of Sanskrit epics and Purāṇas, with which Telugu literature begins, had its roots in a religious movement to spread the Aryan culture among the people. This was achieved to a very limited extent only, because the tone and style of Champu Kāvya was beyond the comprehension of the masses, even when read to them. So it remained essentially the literature of the educated. With the growth of time, the divergence between the literary and popular language became very marked. Literature became the exclusive possession of a select few, of considerable learning. The poet ceased to write even for the educated, but only for the pandit. The problem of bringing to the average man the heritage of the past was, however, not left unsolved. The desideratum of a popular literature, in a country where the generality of society is illiterate, is a simplicity of style and substance, an appealing rhythm, an easy swing of movement, which renders what is heard easily memorized. The new literary vehicles for the dissemination of knowledge among the people were found in Dvipada and Śataka. Dvipada means two feet, i.e., a couplet; śataka means a hundred, that is a cento of verses. Though primarily literary forms, they have by association come to signify a type of literature intended for popular use, different and distinguishable from the epic and the kāvya. When released from the necessity of translating from Sanskrit, the Telugu poet naturally turned to these two modes as most suitable to his native genius, and best adopted for self-expression.

Dvipada Literature. Nanniah employed a metre called *taruvōja*, which consisted of two easily separable halves, balanced by a central pause. We may say that the lines almost invite the reader to bisect them. If we do so and arrange the two halves one below the other, we get something like dvipada. It is necessary to observe both *Yati* and *Prasa*[1] for dvipada. In flexibility and simplicity it resembles the *anushtupa* metre in Sanskrit.

The three great epics have been put into dvipada:

Valmīki Rāmāyaṇa, by Buddha Rāzu.
Rāmāyaṇa, by Raṅganātha.
Uttara Rāmāyaṇa, by Kāchavibhudu and Vittal Rāju.
Bhārata, by Timmakavi.
Bhāgavata, by Kōnēru Kavi.

Śrīnātha's *Palnāti Vīra Charitra* is in this metre. Pālakuriki Somanātha and Madiki Siṁganna are among other writers in this field.

Sataka Literature. From about the twelfth century onwards, we have a broadening stream of śatakas, forming a parallel movement to the kāvya literature. It is estimated that there are about six hundred śatakas so far recovered. Of these only a few are translations or adaptations; the rest are original.

There are some śatakas in Telugu in which the hundred verses are divided into ten groups of ten verses each called *daśakas*. This daśaka division was probably adopted from Prākṛit. However, the standard form consists of a hundred self-complete stanzas. The characteristic feature of the śataka is the *makuta*, or crown, that is, the last word of the stanza, which consists of the name of the person or the deity to whom the preceding lines are addressed. This makuta determines the metre to be employed and thus shapes the structure of the verse.

The themes of the śataka are either outpourings of devotion or the teaching of moral truths; occasionally, humorous reflections on current events and contemporary personalities. Of the six hundred śatakas, more then three-fourths relate to religious and moral teachings. Śaivites and Vaishṇavites have resorted to the śataka, both for propagandistic and devotional purposes. Almost all the great writers have one

[1] See p. 40.

or two śatakas associated with their names. Śataka literature had its beginning in the twelfth century, its zenith in the seventeenth, its widest range in the eighteenth and nineteenth centuries. The earliest śataka we have is *Vṛishādipa Śataka*, by Pālakuriki Somanātha, in 1180. Of almost the same status is *Sumati Śataka*, whose authorship is not certain, though it is generally attributed to Peddana.

Vemana is the prince of śataka writers. Vemana was an Advaitic mystic, a *sannyāsī* who has renounced the world. His birthplace is uncertain, though claims have been made for Kondavīdu, in the Ceded Districts, and Kāturu, a village where his tomb exists; nor can we fix his date, even approximately. Various suggestions have been made, but none on convincing grounds. It is probable that he lived in the beginning of the fifteenth century. He is the greatest moral teacher of the Āndhras. For well-nigh five centuries his *Śataka* has been the text-book of morals for Telugu boys, and a better book cannot be asked for. The *Vemana Śataka* is of a very high literary order. Each stanza is a casket containing a simple moral truth. The idea is never carried beyond a single stanza. The first two lines contain the picture, the next two state the moral. The order is sometimes reversed. Every truth is incarnated in a suitable figure, so apt and just that the mind finds it difficult to separate them. The verses are easily memorized and the rhythm lingers in the memory without effort. The *Śataka* embodies much practical wisdom, shrewd judgment, and kindly advice. It is interesting to note that one verse is a fairly literal translation of Matt. 5 : 43–44[1] and Luke 6 : 33–35, and a third one embodies the Pauline injunction in Rom. 12 : 20, 'If thine enemy hungers, feed him.'

Of devotional śatakas, *Sarveśvara Sataka*, by Yadhā Vākkula Annayya; *Kalahasteśvara Śataka*, by Dhūrjati; *Dāsarathi Śataka*, by Kancherla Gopanna, the celebrated Rāma Bhakta of Bhadrachellam and a disciple

[1] Matt. 5 : 43-44, 'Ye have heard that it hath been said, Thou shalt love thy neighbour, and hate thy enemy. But I say unto you, Love your enemies; bless them that curse you; do good to them that hate you.'

of Kabir; and *Kavi Choudappa Śataka* are among the most popular.

Allied to dvipada and śataka is *daṇḍaka*, (rhapsody of praise), consisting of alliterative phrases permitting a rapid and impetuous outflow with a short prayer at the end. Composed in a single gaṇa, the daṇḍakas are half-sung, half-recited. Not infrequently, the daṇḍakas relate to the majesty, power, and justice of the deity. Wonder, fear, and horror are the sentiments expressed.

Sacred and Secular Music. In India, music is the handmaid of worship. Praises are sung, prayers are intoned, *bhajans* always performed to the accompaniment of musical instruments. Thus it happens that a considerable portion of popular devotional literature is intended to be sung, and is called *geyamulu.* This is not subject to the restraint of prosody, though it keeps to a rough measure. *Kīrtans, kṛitīs, harikathas* belong to this order.

The kīrtans of Tyāgarāja are of the highest spirituality. They breathe a spirit of fervid devotion, simple faith and reliance on Providence. Women, too, have contributed to this literature. *Melukolupulu*, Songs of the Dawn; *Mangaḷahratulu*, Songs of Festivity; *Lālipātalu*, Songs of the Cradle—all contain much true poetry.

There are in Telugu what are called *Jāvaḷis* (Songs of Love) which are looked down upon, as they are sung by public women. But, prejudice apart, the jāvaḷis merit being ranked as high-class poetry. Nowhere, in the whole region of Telugu literature, do we come across the secret longing of love so beautifully expressed. The kāvya writers have debased Śṛingāra Rāsa by identifying it with the cruder erotic sentiment of physical attraction. In the jāvaḷis the same theme has received a more subtle, refined and delicate treatment. Here we find the aroma of longing, the alternate elation and dejection of lovers, set to soft music touched with pathos of a type now made familiar to the western reader in Tagore's *Gardener.*

Prose. We have already seen that, in the South, prose has been extensively used as a medium of popular education. Another use for prose is found in devotional literature in the shape of *vinnapamulu*, or petitions, which resemble the prayers in the Prayer Book of the Church of England. Some of them rise to a high level of thought and diction.

It is much to be regretted that this popular literature has not received the attention it merits. Orthodox critics look down upon it as literature of an inferior class. This judgment will not be endorsed by the modern student. Most of it exists in the form of oral literature, not yet reduced to print. When the industry of the research scholar makes it available for the critic to sift and winnow, it will be found that this literature, scorned by the pandit, looked down upon by the learned, is the true heritage of the Āndhras—their characteristic contribution to the commonwealth of letters—their true *Gītānjali*.

X

WOMEN POETS

It is a pleasing reflection that there is no sex disqualification in the republic of letters. In the Telugu country, as elsewhere, Saraśvatī is justified of her daughters. The condition of society, the prejudices of the age, and the customs of the country, no doubt made it difficult for women to obtain the recognition they merited. Nevertheless, Telugu literature has its women poets..

The influence of women on literature is greater than the number of women poets would lead us to expect. They were patrons of letters when in power, as in the case of Rudramma, the Kākatīya queen. In the humbler rôle of silent sympathisers and gentle critics, their kindly help has always been with us. Many a poet has found hope and encouragement in the knowledge that, invisible to the eye, somewhere behind the *purdah*, are ears straining to hear his poems. Tradition has handed down many memories of cultured women whose help has been the inspiration of our poets.

There is a story of the Āndhra king, Śatavāhana, who was asked by his wife in Sanskrit not to splash water on her while they were engaged in water sports. The king, ignorant of Sanskrit, understood the word *modaka* to mean sweetmeats. His ignorance raised a laugh against him. Stung by the reproach, he set himself to study and in due time became the author of *Bṛihat Kathā Mañjari.* The impression of high culture in the royal household finds confirmation in the conditions prevailing in Kṛishṇadevarāya's zenana.

Then, there is the well-known incident of Potana. While engaged in composing the *Bhāgavata*, one day, he could not get the right line to finish a verse, try as he would. He left the manuscript with his daughter and went out, in the hope that inspiration might come in the open fields. He found, on his return, much to his surprise, the line correctly filled up. There is no need to invent a superfluous miracle, as tradition has done, when we can easily see the timely helper in his daughter.

Equally suggestive is the story of Pinavīranna and his *Jaimini Bhārata.*[1] There, again, we can easily guess that Saraśvatī was not the goddess, but a lady friend of the poet, to whom we owe the *Bhārata*, which we place to the credit of Pinavīranna.

Of the women poets handed down to us by tradition, we may mention the following:

1. Kuppamma, the daughter of Nārāyaṇa Bhaṭ, the friend and helper of Nanniah in his Vaidikī Movement, is said to have been a poetess of merit.

2. Of the same name is the daughter of Budda Rāzu, (1230–40), collaborator with Raṅganātha of *Dvipada Rāmāyaṇa*, who is said to have composed stanzas of touching pathos about her own sorrows as a young widow—which were incorporated by Ayyalarāju Rāmabhadriah in his *Sakala Kathā Sāra Saṅgraha* in the context of Damayantī's sorrow when parted from her husband.

3. Kummari Molla (1509–30), a potter-woman, is the author of the *Molla Rāmāyaṇa*, which has taken its place among the standard works of our literature; indeed, of all the *Rāmāyaṇas*, Molla's is the most widely read and popular. The general high level of her composition, as a whole, entitles her to be ranked with our best poets.

4. Mohanāṅgi, the daughter of Kṛishṇadevarāya, is the author of a Śṛingāra Prabandha, called *Marīchi Pariṇaya*, which she submitted in the full court to the criticism of the poets, who declared it to be a kāvya of merit. Though the book is not now extant, its existence is well attested. That she was passionately fond of good poetry, and that she was a keen judge of merit, is illustrated by the story of her purchase of a verse sold by the indigent poet,

[1] See above p. 67.

Sankuśala Nṛisiṁhakavi,[1] whom she was instrumental in introducing to her father.

5. Muddupaḷaṇi (1765–), a courtesan attached to the court of Pratāpasinha, of Tanjore, composed in flowing, felicitous rhymes a kāvya, *Rādhikā Svantam*, also known as *Eḷadevīya*. This work, like others of the Southern school, is marred by bad taste and utter lack of decency.

6. Tarikonda Venkamma (1839–) composed many kāvyas, of which *Bhāgavata* in dvipada, *Rāja Yogasāra* and *Venkatāchala Mahātya* are important. Her poems, full of elevated sentiments, are an eloquent protest against the debased literary tastes of the day.

7. Subhadramma (1781–) wrote some śatakas and daṇḍakas, of which *Kesava Śataka* and *Kṛishṇa Śataka* may be mentioned.

8. We find another group of women poets in the nineteenth century:

Bandi Bapamma (1850–), wrote *Mināksḥī Śataka.*

Ratnāmba (1870 ?–), wrote *Venkatarāmaṇa Śataka.*

Chelikāni Chellāyama (1900–), wrote *Pārthasārathī Śataka*, *Jānakī Sataka.*

[1] See above, p. 76.

XI

CHRISTIAN AND MUHAMMADAN POETS

Christian Poets

We have two poets, belonging to the seventeenth and eighteenth centuries A.D., respectively, who have written kāvyas on Christian subjects—Piṇgaḷi Erranārya, and Mangaḷagiri Ānandakavi. Both of them were Brahmins—the former attached to a Reddy family, and the latter to a Brahmin family of affluence. Though it is doubtful whether they were formal members of the Christian Church, it is probable that they were followers of Christ from within the Hindu community.

Piṇgaḷi Ellanaryudu (1602) is the author of *Tobhya Charitra*, otherwise known as *Sarveśvara Mahātya.* He informs the reader that through the grace of his guru, Sarabha Nāradhya, he learned the eightfold composition. In an introductory stanza he mentions the important Śaivite saints and poets to whom he offers the customary praises. The book was written at the instance of Thumma Rāyapa Reddi, a petty prince of Baktavāda, in Kondavīdu. In the prologue further details are given as to the circumstances under which he composed the kāvya. Obala Reddi, father of Kondā Reddi, received orally from his āchārya, Sanjivanādha Swāmi, an account of the life of Saint Thomas, which was subsequently reduced to writing. This appears to be the basis for the poet's kāvya.

Mangaḷagiri Ānandakavi (1750). About the middle of the eighteenth century, this poet wrote *Vedānta Rasāyana* and *Anuruddha Charitra.* *Vedānta Rasāyana* is a kāvya in four cantos dedicated to Nidimāmiḷḷa Dāsayāmātya, a member of an influential family which has adopted the

Christian faith. K. Vīresalingam judges the poet to be a writer of very high eminence, worthy to be placed among the best poets of his century.

The author approaches the subject in a devotional frame of mind and gives a clear and succinct account of the life of Christ. The teachings of Jesus are not much referred to. Of the miracles, a few prominent ones are chosen—the raising of Lazarus, the cure of the blind. The Nativity stories and the events of Passion Week are narrated in detail. In the prelude, there is a disquisition on the attributes of God and in the epilogue a discourse on the means of grace. The author shows intimate acquaintance with the scriptures and the rites of the Christian Church. The kāvya is remarkable as the solitary instance in which a Hindu bhakta, saturated with the thought-forms of his own country, has reverently undertaken to proclaim the life of Christ to the world.

The nature of the theme and the necessity of conveying a correct impression of the life of the foreign Guru brings out the best in the author. In handling thought-forms evidently not familiar to the Hindu mind, he shows considerable ability. For example, the phrase 'The lamb that taketh away the sin' is translated without the figure, as *Kalmasha Paritrāṇa* (Remover of Sins). Throughout, we come across touches of fervent Eastern imagination. 'The Holy One,' he says, 'yielding up his spirit, let fall the head on his breast, as the friend of the lotus drops behind the hill of the evening.' In one respect the book stands out as a class apart. The language is chaste and the imagery chastened. The exuberance of fancy, excess of alliteration and complexity of structure, characteristic of kāvya, are all rigorously excluded. We feel in this book the earnestness of the bhakta approaching a subject too precious to indulge in the arts of mere rhetoric.

The recent contributions to Christian literature include the lyrics used in the church—the prominent writer being Choudary Purushottam; and the devotional works of Rāja Bhujanga Rao, whose versification of the New Testament is perhaps the first attempt to present the scriptures of the Christians in a simple, appealing Telugu style.

Muhammadan Poets.

As pointed out,[1] there have been one or two Muhammadan rulers who were patrons of Telugu literature. But, curiously enough, there were no Muhammadan writers till modern times. Among contemporary writers, Ummar Āli Shah is a solitary instance of the Muhammadan poet. One, Gaṅganapalli Hussain, a Muhammadan Vedantist, is the author of *Hussain Dāsu Śataka* and *Kumati Śataka.*

[1] See above p 84

XII

THE MODERN PERIOD (1850-1925)

THE advent of the British brought the Āndhra culture into contact with the vitalizing influences of Western literatures and arts. The intelligentsia acquired a knowledge of English literature. Under its influence, literary tastes are changing, and literary ideals undergoing radical transformations. New ideals challenge attention and evoke enthusiasm; new watchwords are springing up. On one side, love for the vernaculars is being intensified; on the other side, there is a growing, almost a petulant, impatience with the old forms and ideals. The mutual interpretation of the two cultures has hardly begun. How the genius of the race is going to react remains to be seen. A new power has entered our literary life, and it is too early to forecast the possibilities of this conjunction. Meanwhile the air is thick with revolutionary creeds, anarchic tendencies, reactionary obscurantism. The twentieth century is vibrant with literary activity. It is only possible to note a few of the striking features. Broadly speaking, the activities fall under three heads: (1) Critical. (2) Creative. (3) Traditional.

Under the first head fall (*a*) literary controversies, (*b*) literary research, (*c*) literary criticism. Under the second, we have the drama, the novel, new prose, new poetry, short stories, the literature of knowledge, literary magazines, etc. Under the third head are grouped the activities which carry forward the traditional literature and use traditional methods. It is not possible, even if it were advisable, to refer to contemporary writers in detail. We propose to restrict ourselves to general tendencies and movements, referring to prominent writers only by way of illustration.

CRITICAL ACTIVITIES

Literary Controversies. One controversy, which has led to an acrimonious battle of words, relates to the rival claims of the literary (grāndika) and colloquial (grāmya) types of Telugu languages. In Telugu, unlike English, the language of literature is separated by a wide (and widening) gulf from the colloquial. Zealous reformers, anxious to make literature the living language of the people, are advocating that the 'pandit language,' with its complicated grammar, stilted style, tawdry ornamentation, and fantastic restraints of slesha and yamaka, shall be replaced by a simpler and more graceful medium. There are extremists on both sides; 'Pharisees' who regard common language as untouchable, and 'Philistines' who would sacrifice all beauty for utility. Between these extremes there is a growing consensus of opinion that it is possible to have a literary medium which is grammatical without being pedantic, and simple without being vulgar or crude.

2. Another controversy relates to the nature and function of literature. Four centuries of devotion to the kāvya type has created an impasse. With the traditional school, language and technique are everything, ideas and inspiration are nothing. The pendulum has now swung to the other side. One school, in its devotion to life, would exclude art from literature. Another school insists that everything Indian should be discarded and everything English should be admired. They have no eye for the genius of their own language. They are anarchists who desire to break down all traditional restrictions. They willingly exchange old lamps for new; priceless tapestries and jewels for the glittering glass of the foreign market. These attempts have produced the most grotesque hybrid patchwork, which has neither the beauty of Telugu nor the vitality of English. A hopeful feature of the situation is the growing number of radical reformers who realise that the mechanical adjustments of cultures will only result in incongruous medley, and consequently stand for a living fusion of culture in the realm of the spirit.

Literary Research. A few of the many lines of activity pursued by research scholars may be here indicated.

1. *The Recovery of Lost Literature.* Mānavalli Rāmakṛishṇiah has scoured the country with a view to ascertain whether there was any pre-Sanskrit Telugu literature before Nanniah. He has collected a considerable number of hitherto unpublished manuscripts, which, whether they prove the existence of pre-Nanniah literature or not, are a valuable addition to the existing stock of books. His discovery and publication of Nannechodu's *Kumāra Sambhava* is a literary event of capital importance. The Āndhra Ṣāhitya Parishad has for its credit the recovery of many hundreds of volumes belonging to the Southern school of Telugu literature. The Government Oriental Library represents the work done by the State in this connection. The valuable collections by Dr. Brown and Col. Mackenzie deserve grateful recognition.

2. *The Consolidation of the Results of Research.* This has been done by working the raw materials supplied by various departments of research into a coherent whole in the shape of histories of literature and lives of poets. Mr. K. Vīresalingam's *Lives of Telugu Poets* (*Āndhra Kavula Charitra*) is a standard work of reference. It is a monument of patient research and sound scholarship. *Biographies of Telugu Poets* (*Kavijīvitamulu*), by Guruzāda Śrīrāmamurti, though less reliable, contains a wealth of information about Telugu poets. Vanguri Subbā Rao's *History of Telugu Literature* (*Āndhra Vāṅgmaya Charitra*) is a study in literary evolution of considerable merit and originality.

3. *Perpetuation of Oral Literature.* As we have already indicated, pre-Nanniah literature of considerable antiquity, forming the indigenous Deśī literature, still exists in the shape of songs and stories, which have not yet been printed. The value of oral literature is gradually being realised. T. Rājagopala Rao has made investigations in Deśī metre and has acquired a collection of nursery rhymes. Vetūri Prabhākara Śāstrī has already published a volume of Chatudhāra poems and has ready for publication *Songs of the Playfield*. Vanguri Subbā Rao has made a valuable contribution in his *Śataka Poets*. Nandī Rāju Chelapati Rao has brought out a collection of songs of festivity.

Folklore is being slowly gathered aud published piecemeal.

4. A fourth line of activity relates to the exploring of Prākṛit in order to find the evolution of the Telugu language and to determine the influence of Jainism and Buddhism on our literature.

5. *Comparative Studies.* The grammars and vocabularies of Dravidian languages are being explored, with a view to ascertain their mutual relation and obligations. B. Sheshagiri Row and Gidugu Rāmamūrti are conspicuous in this field.

Literary Criticism. The primary function of criticism is to exhibit the work of an author in the best light, with a view to bring out the graces of his style and the quality of his creative art. Constructive criticism of this nature is now being pursued along two lines of activity:

(1) A co-ordination of the labours of epigraphists, palæologists and historians is being made, with a view to recover the historical background, and the spirit and atmosphere of the age. The names of Jayanti Rāmiah and Kommarāju Lakshmaṇa Rao Pantulu stand out prominent in this field.

(2) Critical editions of classical authors are being prepared, with elaborate introductions, containing discussions on the date, the social setting of the poem, merits of style and the correct reading of the text.

2. Another direction in which criticism is making itself felt is the evaluation of literary tendencies and claims. The regulative function of criticism is no less important than the constructive. According to the orthodox tradition, a place of primacy is given to the kāvya type, and the literary outlook it implies. Modern criticism, equipped with a knowledge of other literatures, is challenging this position. The assault against kāvya is led by the radical critics of this generation. The ethics of Śṛingārarāsa, the utility of ornamentation, and the worth of slesha have all come under fire. A trans-valuation of literary values is taking place. Two brilliant works recently published deserve mention: *Kavitatva Vichāraṇa*, by C. R. Reddy; *Śataka Kavulu*, by Vanguri Subbā Rao.

The latter is an attempt to restore popular literature to its true place. Among the critics of the day, Vedam Venkatarāya Śāstrī, Vetūri Prabhākara Śāstrī and the Kasī Bhatla Brothers command respect for their learning, critical acumen and sympathy for new developments in literature. They realise that a critical appreciation of our literary heritage is the only enlightened safeguard against revolution on one side and reaction on the other.

Literary criticism in its truest sense, namely, estimating and exhibiting the true excellence of a poet, is not new to Telugu literature. It is a long-standing custom to introduce in the introductory portion ślokas praising the work of the great poets. These ślokas are really models of literary criticism, expressing in neat and compact phrases the true estimate of the poet, with remarkable insight. We give two instances, supposed to have been stanzas addressed to Śrīnātha and to Kākamāni Mūrti, respectively:

(1) 'Thou canst compose now like Bhīma Kavi (p. 58 f.) in words of power, now like Nanniah (p. 42 f.) in the glory of two languages (Telugu and Sanskrit), now like Tikkanna (pp. 44 ff.) in verses glistening with rasas, now after the manner of Prabandha Parameśvāra (p. 48), in stanzas of felicitous word and phrase.'

(2) 'The word-weaving magic of Peddana (p. 72), the honeyed sweetness of Timmanna (p. 74), the majesty of expression of Pāṇḍuraṅga Rāmakṛishṇa (p. 83) are thine.'

CREATIVE ACTIVITIES

The greatest change that is coming over our literary outlook is not so much the work of conscious criticism, as the effect of the time-spirit affecting the basis of literary life. The decadence of poetry, patent during the last four centuries, has been due to the ebbing away of vital energies from literature—a fact often masked behind elaborate word-architecture. The primary cause of this anæmia has been the segregation of the poet from the vital currents of life. He lost touch with realities, and lived in an artificial world of his own making. The pandit, the grammarian, and the rhetorician presented the poet with an artificial system of cardboard men and women gaudily painted, standardized emotions, and stereotyped figures of speech and thought, unchanged through long ages. But now the new life has broken into this strongly barricaded enclosure, and has liberated the spirit of poetry from the prison-house of fixed ideas. The re-animation of fading energies, the re-kindling of hope—in short, the recovery of youth and vigour—are among the spiritual gains of this contact with world-thought. The literary output springing from the new spirit may be classified under three heads:

1. The Literature of Knowledge.
2. The Literature of Union.
3. The Literature of Rejuvenation.

The Literature of Knowledge. A craving for translation is a congenital impulse in Telugu literature. We began with an era of translations, and we are in the midst of an active recrudescence of the phenomenon. Ever since Mr. Vīresalingam translated Lamb's *Tales from Shakespeare*, the appetite for translations has become voracious. Sanskrit drama, Bengali poetry, French novels, Russian tales, science, art and history are included in the range of translations. Another branch of this type of literature is the preparation of books of reference. The Āndhra Parishad is compiling a new Telugu Dictionary called *Sūrya Rāya Nigantu*, after the name of the Rāja of Pitapur, who is financing the undertaking. The *Vijñāna Chandrikā* Series was started with the object of bringing to the Telugu reader the wealth of world-culture. Mr. C. Vīrabhadra Rao's *History of the Āndhras* (*Āndhrula Charitra*) and *Āndhra Sarvasvamu* (a Telugu Encyclopædia), edited by the late Mr. K. Lakshmaṇa Rao, are among the most notable publications of this series.

The Literature of Union. Under this class fall new modes of activity in Telugu literature, such as the drama, novel, short story, and new poetry. This literature is born at the confluence of two streams of thought, East and West, and is controlled by English-educated young men, who look at the heritage of the past from a new standpoint.

1. **The Drama.** Though drama as a department of Telugu literature is of recent origin, acted plays have existed for a long time. Cruder forms of drama were in vogue in the form of *Pagati-Veshamulu* (Daylight Plays) and *Vīdhi-*

nāṭakamulu (Street Plays). Stage-craft must have attained some development, as we find Śrīnātha mentioning the name Butchigadu as a celebrated actor of female parts in his day. Piṇgaḷi Sūranna's *Prabhāvati Pradyumnamu* (p. 79), if it can be taken to reflect prevailing conditions, throws interesting light on the acting and the staging of the drama.

The earliest drama in the Telugu language is Vallabhā Mātya's *Kṛidābhi Rāmamu* (Street Scenes) at the Imperial capital, Warangal. The author says that he had seen a woman acting portions of *Palnāti Vīra Charitra.* The next set of dramas are of the eighteenth century. They are Bālasaraśvatī's *Raṅgakaumudi* and Kaṁkanti Pāpa Rāju's *Vishṇu Māya Vilāsa.* The Southern school was more prolific in dramas, but it is doubtful whether any of them have a claim to be regarded as literature.

The origin of the modern Telugu drama is traceable to the influence of the plays of Shakespeare, often enacted in India, and the impulse given by the advent of the Dhārvada Nātaka Company and Parsi theatricals. The plays fall under the three classes: (1) Adaptations from Sanskrit and English; (2) Social Satire; (3) Historical Drama.

With the exception of one or two plays, most of them are a mediocre type. There seems to be a feud between the playwright and the producer. The popular dramas have no literary value and literary dramas are not popular.

Purāṇic Dramas. Purāṇas supply an inexhaustible store of material. Here, too, as elsewhere, a beginning is made with translations. Prominent translators from Sanskrit are: (1) Paravastu Rangāchārlu, *Śakuntalā.* (2) Kokkonda Venkataratnam Pantulu, *Narakāsura Vijaya.* (3) Veddādi Śubbārāyudu, *Mallika Māruta, Veṇī Saṁhāra, Sakuntalā, Vikrama Urvasīya.*

Other dramas belonging to this order are: *Mṛichakatika, Ratnāvali* and *Droupati Vastrāpaharaṇa.* In the present decade, these have been replaced by plays which are independent adoptions of Purāṇic stories. D. Kṛishṇamācharlu is a popular author of many Purāṇic dramas, of which *Chitra Naliyam* has had a great run. In point of literary merit the plays of Vedam Venkata Rāya Śastrī are amongst the best.

Social Satire. Mr. Vīresalingam has written light farces, more or less of the nature of interludes, which are very popular. In these, social follies and foibles are held up to ridicule in comic sketches written in a light vein. Guruzāda Apparao, who wrote *Kanyā Sulka* (dealing with the scandal of the dowry system), and Pānuganti Lakshminarasiṁha Rao, who wrote *Kantābharaṇam*, are prominent writers of satirical plays.

Historical Drama. A writer above the ordinary level is K. Śrinivasa Rao, the leader of the historic drama. *Prithivī Rāja* and *The Fall of Vijayanagar* are the most popular of his plays. Both of them are tragedies—a type not represented in the Indian dramas. *The Fall of Vijayanagar* is a study in race conflict. Rāma Rāzu, the last of the Vijayanagar kings, had an illegitimate son by a Muhammadan woman, whom he brings up as his own son and entrusts him with the command of his army in the fateful battle of Taḷikota. The hero is in love with a Muhammadan girl, a captive of war, who seeks to revenge the insult offered to her by the king and incites him to go over to the enemy. The hero is in the grip of a great struggle. The call of his race and of love points one way, but the call of duty and parental affections urge in the opposite direction. Under the stress of a great emotional conflict he turns mad on the battlefield and, after killing his father, commits suicide. Of the other historical plays the following deserve mention:

Roshanara, by K. Subbā Rao.

Pratāparudra, by V. Venkata Rāya Śāstrī.

Bobbili Battle, by Śrīpāda Kṛishṇa Mūrti.

Sārangadhara, a play of questionable morals and execrable taste, disgraces the stage.

2. **The Novel.** The novel is unrepresented in old Telugu literature and owes its birth to the influence of its English prototype. *Kādambarī*, a type of metrical romance, copied from the Sanskrit, is the nearest approach to the novel. The novel, though fast becoming popular, is still in its initial stages of development. Most of them are second-rate copies or adaptations from English. The original productions are crude, hybrid patchworks of immature

workmanship. The historic and domestic novel is represented by translations from Bengali, mainly from Bankim Chandra Chattopādhyaya and Romesh Chandra Dutt. The credit of being the pathfinder in this field belongs to Mr. Vīresalingam, whose *Rāja Śekhara Charitra*, adapted from the *Vicar of Wakefield*, is the earliest novel. The detective novel is just making its appearance, and it is too early to predict its future. In the construction of the plot and development of interest and vividness of style Ch. Lakshmīnarasiṁhan stands head and shoulders over the writers of the day.

3. **Satire.** In the eighteenth and the nineteenth centuries A.D., two poets became conspicuous by their satirical writings. Their humour, never polished, often malicious, and occasionally descending to vulgarity, was intended to hurt. Jaggakavi's *Chandra Rekhā Vilāpam*, though marred by long stretches of low humour, is of a better type. He holds up to ridicule the life of the idle-rich—the zamindars of the day—their vanity, vulgarity and crude immorality. He was a master of invective. *Ravaṇa Dommīyamu*, known as *Laṅkā Vijaya*, is an instance of satire after the manner of the *Dunciad*. Parody is represented by Gīrata.

In the twentieth century, following the example of English humorists, a new type of literature has come into existence. Mr. Vīresalingam's prahasanas lead the way for social satire. Genial and kindly, pointed but never painful, the author's light farces are models to be followed. A worthy successor to him is Pānuganṭi Lakshmīnarasiṁham, whose *Sākshi* (Spectator) is an example of clean, sparkling humour, which seeks to kill social vices without cruelty.

4. **New Prose.** Up to the eighteenth century, verse was the universal medium of Telugu literature. Such prose as existed occurred in parenthetical snatches, introduced as a literary device. The eighteenth century prose was more a creature of necessity than of literary perception. As a result of modern controversies, there is a clearer delineation of the province of prose and verse, and a clearer perception of the possibilities of prose. Modern prose, like Nanniah's, is simpler and more malleable than

the 'high prose' of the kāvya period. Mr. Vīresalingam is the pioneer, and Mr. P. Chinniah Sūri sets the model of perspicuity and grace in his *Pañchaṭanṭra*.

5. **New Poetry.** The most prominent of recent tendencies in literature, which holds the promise of a great future, is the 'New Poetry.' Unlike the new drama and the new novel, it is not imitative. Though profoundly influenced by Bengali literature on one side, and English on the other, it has neither borrowed the substance nor copied the form from outside. It is the product of literary tendencies long lying dormant, now awakened to activity by the impetus of new forces from outside. The significance of the new poetry lies in the fact that it marks a return to Deśī type of literature—the native element in which the Āndhra mind can flower and bear fruit. From the twelfth century onwards our poetry has been a wanderer in the realm of Sanskrit culture. The 'New Poetry' marks the joyful home-coming of the prodigal. Much of it is strewn broadcast in contemporary magazines, and hence it is difficult to assess correctly its value and tendency. As far as can be judged, it is expressing itself in lyric and sonnet. Part of it reflects a spirit of simple fellowship and communion with nature, and may develop into a Nature School. The honour of being the pioneer in this line of development belongs to Rāyaprolu Subbā Rao. The Sāhiti Samiti, a literary association started for the purpose of cultivating the 'New Poetry,' contains among its members most of the prominent poets of this school. D. Ramireddi's *Kṛishīvaludu* is a welcome departure from worn-out paths. It is a description of the life of the agriculturist, of the procession of the seasons, and the glory of the harvest. Some of the lyrics are after the fashion of Shelley's *Skylark*. The prominent feature is its suggestiveness. Behind the obvious value there is a suggestion of spiritual meaning. The setting sun, somehow, suggests the passing away of the soul; the music of the bangle yields some illusive song of the spirit. *Venki Songs*, by N. Subbā Rao, sums up the elusive charm of simple imagery, hinting depths of meaning. In *Venki Songs* the new poetry of this decade reaches its high-water mark.

6. **The Short Story.** We have in Telugu literature the didactic fable represented by *Pañchaṭanṭra*, prose romances represented by *Daśakumāra Charitra*, stories after the manner of *Arabian Nights* represented by *Madana Kāma Rāju* stories and *Suka Saptati*, tales of wonder represented by *Simhāsana Dvātrimiska* stories, and tales in verse represented by *Navanātha Charitra* and *Dhanābhi Rāmamu*. But the 'short story' in the modern sense is only now making its appearance. The following collection of short stories have already been published:

(1) Pānuganṭi Lakshminarasiṁham Rao, *Suvarṇa Rekhā Kathāvali*.

(2) Mādapati Hānumanta Rao, *Mallikā Gutchamu* (A Bouquet of Jasmin).

(3) Akki Rāju Umākānta, *Trilinga Stories.*

(4) Śrīpāda Subramanya Śāstrī, *Phūladanda* (A Garland of Flowers).

TRADITIONAL ACTIVITIES

Alongside the new poetry the historic tradition of the epic and the kāvya is continued, though under new and vastly changed environment. The poets trained in the old learning, holding allegiance to old idols, are writing kāvyas. These represent the conservative wing of the literary advance. Though not directly influenced by English literature, the new culture is brought to bear upon them in a thousand and one channels of suggestion and contact. Their literary productions are infused with a sense of the new life. The crudities of kāvya outlook are shed, and the ornate style is replaced by a pleasing blend of the softness of the old with the vigour of the new. More attention is paid to the story and less to the description. Harmony and proportion are studied. Of the prominent authors of this school the following may be mentioned:

(1) Tirupati Venkateśvara Kavulu.
(2) Rāmakṛishṇa Kavulu.
(3) Kokkonda Venkataratnam.
(4) Veddādi Sebbārāyudu.
(5) Devulapalli Brothers, of Pithapuram.

Magazines and Newspapers. The printing press, which is pregnant with revolutionary possibilities, has transferred the power of patronage from the king and the zamindar to a reading public. In the past, kings and *sanghams* were the judges of the poet. This is fast changing. The critical function is passing into the hands of newspapers and magazines. It may not be out of place here just to note the more important of the current magazines:

(1) The *Āndhra Patrika.* This premier Telugu daily has played an important part in promoting the revival of letters. It is the supporter of new movements in literature.

(2) The *Āndhra Parishad Patrika* stands for cautious advance in literary reform.

(3) *Bhārati*, a high-class literary magazine, mainly interested in the promotion of research and encouragement of new tendencies in literature.

(4) *Sāhiti* is the exponent of new poetry and specializes in the short story.

(5) *Sārada* focuses literary tendencies and forms a link between the conservative and liberal schools.

(6) *Kaḷā* stands for the correlation of art and literature.

(7) *Saraśvatī* publishes unpublished works in instalments. It is the organ of the conservative school.

(8) *Mañjuvāṇi* (now discontinued), a literary magazine with the same object as *Saraśvatī.*

XIII

RETROSPECT AND PROSPECT

THE history of Telugu literature, as narrated in the previous chapters, has enabled us to trace its development in broad outlines. Starting with the humble beginnings in the Deśī, the normal tenor of development was violently arrested by the inauguration of the Mārgī. The Deśī literature, like the pretty prattling brooks of the countryside, represented the natural outpourings of the simple-hearted indigenous poet. From about the eleventh century A.D. new ambitions have filled the literary vision. The poets have assayed to build an august 'Vidyasāgar,' for which they acquired the necessary engineering skill by arduous apprenticeship to Sanskrit writers. Having built it, they diverted into it the stagnating waters of Sanskrit culture. It is a noble achievement, imposing in its grandeur, though lacking in simplicity. Thenceforward Sanskrit-Telugu literature became the main current, the Deśī surviving by sufferance. Had it been otherwise, had the main line of development been with the Deśī, had Sanskrit been content to play the rôle of a generous sympathiser from outside, instead of being stepmother within the household, we should have had a nobler history to write, and a prouder heritage to commemorate. As it is, Āndhra literature, though wanting in originality and creative energy, is nevertheless varied and beautiful—a heritage of which the Telugu can justly be proud and to which he can always turn for inspiration.

Characteristics. What are the distinguishing features of Telugu literature, as compared with Sanskrit on the one hand, and Dravidian literatures on the other? What individual and characteristic note does it strike? The Telugu poets are not creators but artists. Theirs is not the supreme genius of inspiration, but the secondary excellence of craftsmanship. They are excellent moulders. The moulds and the materials are borrowed; but the art of melting and the cunning of casting is all their own. The images they turn out are the Purāṇic images common to Sanskrit and Dravidian literatures; but the polish of features, the delicacy of pencilling, the deftness of touch is peculiar to Telugu poetic art. The Telugu poets are worshippers of style; and their art is in the refinement of language. It is the dexterity of weaving words, the daintiness of sentiment, sweetness of phrasing that draws their admiration. In technical language, the differentia of Telugu poetry is 'pāka,' the art of melting Sanskrit and Telugu in due proportion and the knack of pouring it into the mould at the right temperature. Telugu poetry is song set to music; symphony and sweetness is its soul. The Telugu poets have grafted the wild Sanskrit onto the crude Dravidian-Telugu stock, and have evolved a luscious literary Telugu, which, like the mango, is unmatched for taste and colour. There is no more beautiful or sweeter language among Indian tongues than the literary Telugu; the guttural harshness of Sanskrit is subdued and the crudeness of Dravidian Telugu sublimated by a judicious blend. The best Telugu poets are those who have learned the secret of this harmonious blend.

Defects. This facility, almost this witchery, of expression has been alike the excellence and ruin of Telugu literature. It rendered it all too easy to separate art from life. This central weakness has prevented Telugu literature from taking its place among the great literatures of the world. The Telugu poets, though conscientious and capable artists, fall short of being creators. They have not given to the world any creations corresponding to Hamlet, Shylock, Jingle, Pickwick, or Sherlock Holmes. In the international assembly of poets' ideal creations, the Āndhra is unrepresented. Life thus divorced from art took its revenge whenever the poets ventured into paths of independence, by striking them with confusion. With regard to form and language, the instinct of the Telugu poets is unerring, and their taste cultivated. But in the realm of ideation, their instincts were perverted, taste crude, judgment clouded. In the indictment against Telugu poetry there are many counts, and all of them flow from this dissociation of art from life. The poets copied Sanskrit literature, not at its best, but just when it was decadent; not from the masterpieces of *Vaidarbhi*, but from the artificial elaboration of Gauda style. It is a humiliating reflection that they translated *Śakuntalā* as a kāvya. They avoided the drama and admired the kāvya. Their adoration of the kāvya stamps them all over with literary ineptitude. They neglected the natural beauties of the Deśī and cultivated the tawdry elaborations of the Mārgī. They exalted the sickening excesses of *Śṛingāra* over the subtle charms of the *Jāvaḷi*. The kāvya heroes are not strong men of action and achievement, but psychopathic perverts grovelling in eroticism. *Chitra Kavitva* is literary acrobacy. The love of slesha is but a primitive taste. All these defects, present in the shape of incipient tendencies in all except the major poets, become increasingly patent from the time of the Ashṭadiggajās; till at last in the seventeenth, eighteenth and nineteenth centuries, the movements of literature, like the dance of a paralytic, are stiff, uncouth, painful alike to perform and to witness. Here lies also the striking paradox in Telugu literature. The age of translations was really the age of freedom, and the so-called age of independence (the kāvya age) ushered in the period of bondage. When the poet borrowed the substance from Sanskrit, he retained the freedom of art and expression; but when he borrowed the art from Sanskrit, he lost the freedom of thought.

The mischief of excessive preoccupation with art and technique, to the neglect of life, did not stop with these disastrous consequences to literary thought, taste and judgment, but has induced a moral outlook in the poets which is detrimental to all true progress. In the first place, the poets became indifferent to what they borrowed and where they borrowed it from, so long as they were able to cast it in a sweet musical medium. Since it was easier to borrow themes from outside, than carve them out of raw life, they became chronic mendicants. They borrowed from Sanskrit literature in the Purāṇa Yuga, from Sanskrit rhetoricians in the Prabandha Yuga, from each other in Andhakāra Yuga, from all and sundry in the Nava Yuga—all this, when the life within and without clamoured for poetic expression. Hence, Telugu literature reflects very little of Āndhra life, history, culture, scenery. In the second place, the constant association with what was deemed to be a superior culture, Sanskrit, bred in the poet a tendency to develop high-brow literature, contemptuous of common life and simple emotions; and with the snobbery of parvenus, they called Dvipada 'an old hag,' and barely tolerated Śataka. The neglect of a life which was their own, the hankering after a life which was others', was the moral retribution of the severing of life and art.

Telugu literature is a flaming red symbol of warning against dissociation of life from art in literature. It is a literary transgression of the first magnitude to legislate for life, and maintain, as the authorities on poetics have done, that there are only nine 'rasas.'[1] Life is so various, mysterious, elusive that we have to say that the rasas are ninety times nine. Love is not Śṛingāra, the mephitic inhalations of lust alone. There are a thousand tenses and moods for love—the love that weeps, laughs, prattles, rollics, smiles, kills, immolates. Poetry must ally itself with the mystery of life in all its ceaseless manifestations. To force life into the cast-iron systems of grammarians and rhetoricians is to forfeit all claims to inspiration. The real danger to literature does not arise from anarchists—they damage but the body. The enemies are of the household, the pandit and the pedant—for they hurt the soul.

The Future. The future of Telugu literature depends largely upon the capacity of the new generation of poets to escape from the bondage of the kāvya ideal and outlook. Fortunately, there are unmistakable signs in the literature of the last three decades that the emancipation is already being effected. A union of life and art is being established anew. Through contact with Western literatures and the

[1] See above p. 35.

emergence of new social and political ideals, a fresh and truer conception of poetry is coming into vogue. It is realised that the poet is something more than the maker of verses, however beautiful. The poet is the seer, who sees life anew. The poet is the visionary, who imparts his visions to the reader.

The reaction against kāvya may carry the poet to the other extreme. If great art alone does not make noble literature, neither does great thought alone. Doubtless, life is the major partner; but art has a vital interest. Quarried stones must be cut and polished. The neglect of form is only a passing phase. If our poets lay firm hold of the simple truth that true literature is the *artistic expression of life*, there is no need to be pessimistic of the future. The fecundity of the last few decades inspires hope for the future. A literature that has survived four centuries of kāvya must have had a charmed life. The love of art is always with the Telugu poets. What literature stands in supreme need of is baptism by full immersion in Āndhra life. Then the modern renaissance may yet add a new chapter to the Telugu literature, which can worthily compare with the glories of the Kavitraya and the grandeur of the Ashṭadiggajās.

INDEX

Titles of books are given in *italics*